Life

4a
Combo Split
Student Book

Paul Dummett
John Hughes
Helen Stephenson

Life Level 4a Combo Split

Paul Dummett

John Hughes

Helen Stephenson

Publisher: Sherrise Roehr

Executive Editor: Sarah T. Kenney

Editorial Assistant: Patricia Giunta

Director of Global Marketing: Ian Martin

Senior Product Marketing Manager:
Caitlin Thomas

Director of Content and Media Production:
Michael Burggren

Production Manager: Daisy Sosa

Senior Print Buyer: Mary Beth Hennebury

Cover Designers: Scott Baker

Cover Image: Jim Richardson / National
Geographic Creative

Compositor: MPS Limited

Cover Image

Gondolas docked by the Piazza San Marcos in
Venice, Italy. *Photograph by Jim Richardson.*

Combo Split A + CD-ROM
ISBN-13: 978-1-305-25739-9

Combo Split A + Online Workbook
ISBN-13: 978-1-305-26437-3

National Geographic Learning/Cengage Learning
20 Channel Center Street
Boston, MA 02210
USA

Cengage Learning is a leading provider of customized learning solutions
with office locations around the globe, including Singapore, the United
Kingdom, Australia, Mexico, Brazil, and Japan. Locate our local office at
international.cengage.com/region

Cengage Learning products are represented in Canada by Nelson
Education, Ltd.

Visit National Geographic Learning online at **NGL.Cengage.com**
Visit our corporate website at **www.cengage.com**

Printed in the United States of America
Print Number: 04   Print Year: 2017

UNIT 1
COLOR

UNIT 2
PERFORMANCE

UNIT 3
WATER

UNIT 4
OPPORTUNITIES

UNIT 5
TRAVEL

UNIT 6
WELLBEING

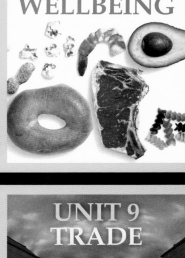

UNIT 7
LIVING SPACE

UNIT 8
WEIRD NEWS

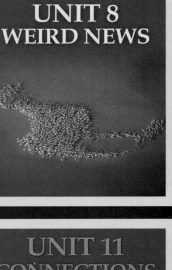

UNIT 9
TRADE

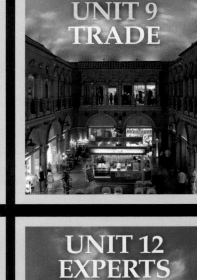

UNIT 10
NO LIMITS

UNIT 11
CONNECTIONS

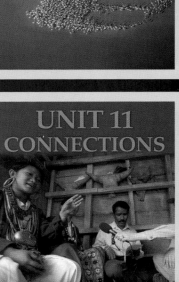

UNIT 12
EXPERTS

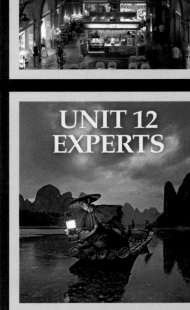

Contents

LISTENING	READING	CRITICAL THINKING	SPEAKING	WRITING
two people doing a quiz about colors and their meaning	an article about how we use color an article about the color red	conclusions	routines and leisure activities personal questions the roles we play	text type: a website profile writing skill: criteria for writing
a radio show about world fusion music	an article about why we dance an article about globalization	sources	new releases performing changes	text type: a profile writing skill: linking ideas (1)
two people talking about what happened next	an interview about underwater discoveries an article about an unforgettable experience	reading between the lines	the first time puzzles it happened to me	text type: a blog post writing skill: interesting language
three young women talking about their future	an article about India's new superhighway an article about the economic boom in China	arguments	predictions planning your work pay and conditions	text type: a cover letter writing skill: formal style
part of a radio show about a wildlife conservationist three conversations about vacation activities	a profile of a wildlife conservationist an article about vacation destinations an article about tourism and conservation	close reading	travel experiences what makes a good vacation green activities	text type: a postcard writing skill: informal style
two people discussing the power of the mind	a news item about traditional dishes a news item about imaginary eating an article about modern lifestyles	language clues	your favorite dish a healthy lifestyle modern life	text type: a formal letter writing skill: explaining consequences

Life around the world

Unit 2 Taiko master

The history of Taiko drumming from its origins in Japan to modern-day San Francisco.

Unit 7 A special kind of neighborhood

Stories from the Mission District of San Francisco.

Unit 8 Killer bees

Discover why killer bees are damaging the future of the Latin American rain forests.

Unit 9 Making a deal

Learn how to bargain in Morocco.

Unit 3 One village makes a difference

Solving the problems of India's water shortage.

Unit 4 Confucianism in China

Learn more about the famous Chinese philosopher Confucius.

San Francisco
USA

Pacific Ocean

Mexico

Panama

Morocco

China

Japan

India

Ethiopia

Gabon

Peru
Bolivia

Argentina

Antarctica

Unit 12 Shark vs. octopus

What happens when a shark and an octopus meet.

Unit 5 A disappearing world

A scientific expedition to record data about the rain forests of the Congo Basin.

Unit 10 High-altitude people

Why research into people living at high altitude gives us a better understanding of human evolution.

Unit 1 Peruvian weavers

A weavers' cooperative managed by the women of Chinchero.

Unit 11 Crossing Antarctica

The amazing story of two women's ambition to ski across Antarctica.

Unit 6 Dangerous dining

Find out why people eat the most dangerous fish on Earth: fugu.

Two girls at a family event in Brunei
Photograph by Adam Hanif

FEATURES

1 Work in pairs. Look at the photo. What do the colors tell you about where the girls are? How do you think they feel?

2 Work in pairs. How do these colors make you feel? What do they make you think of? When do you see them or use them?

red	purple
black	green
yellow	blue
white	gray

3 Discuss these questions with your partner. Are your answers similar or different?

1 What color is your house / your kitchen / your car / your cell phone?
2 What is your favorite color? Why?
3 Which color do you normally wear? Why?

1a Life in color

Reading

1 Read the article *Life in color*. How is color important to the people in the photos?

2 Read the article again and find the following information:

1 three ways we use color
2 one example of each way we use color

3 Work in pairs. Compare your answers from Exercise 2. Then think of examples for the three uses of color from your own culture.

Grammar simple present and present continuous

4 Underline the simple present and circle the present continuous forms in the article. Which verb form do we use for these things?

1 things that are always or generally true?
2 things that are in progress at the time of speaking?
3 things that are regular actions?

> ▶ **SIMPLE PRESENT and PRESENT CONTINUOUS**
>
> **Simple present**
> *The "in" color changes every season.*
> **Present continuous**
> *This fall, women are wearing shades of purple and lilac.*
>
> For more information and practice, see page 156.

A

Huli villager, Papua New Guinea
Photograph by Tim Laman

B

Quechua high-school student, Peru
Photograph by Michael S Lewis

Life in *color*

We live our lives in color from our earliest days. For example, in Western cultures, pink is for baby girls and blue is for baby boys. Color plays a big part in everything we do. We use it both as a badge of identity and a way of expressing our individuality through decoration. And we use different colors to send out very different messages.

IDENTITY People need a sense of group identity. Look at the schoolboy in the photo. From his colorful traditional dress, other people in Peru know he comes from the Quechua community. We wear uniforms at school and work, and we dress in our favorite sports teams' colors to say the same thing: we belong to this group.

DECORATION The Huli villager in the photo is getting ready for a local festival. He's applying the traditional colors of red, black, and white in his own personal pattern. Face painting is an important part of the celebrations, and these days people are starting to experiment with brightly colored synthetic paints as well as traditional hues. In fashion-conscious Western cities, the "in" color changes every season. This fall, for example, women are wearing shades of purple and lilac.

MESSAGES Marketing experts understand the power of color very well. Packaging and labels in eye-catching colors stand out on the supermarket shelf. And companies always select the color of their brand very carefully—a calm blue for a bank you can trust, dark green to suggest quality and sophistication, or brown and green to indicate eco-friendliness.

hue (n) /hju/ a shade of a color
packaging (n) /ˈpækɪdʒɪŋ/ a container for a product

5 Complete the comments with the simple present and present continuous forms of the verbs.

Feng, IT student
We ¹ _____ (dress) casually at my college. But today my tutor ² _____ (wear) bright blue bike shorts! I know everyone ³ _____ (say) IT people are "different," but I think it's a little much!

Leo, finance assistant
My boss often ⁴ _____ (get) crazy ideas. At the moment, we ⁵ _____ (try) out a new color coding system in shades of pink!

Mina, sales assistant
I usually ⁶ _____ (get) take-out for lunch. I ⁷ _____ (not /eat) inside because the bright yellow and red tables are horrible!

▶ **STATIVE VERBS**

We use stative verbs to talk about states. These verbs are not normally used in the continuous form. Some verbs, for example *love*, can have both stative and dynamic meanings.
Jinous loves clothes. Jinous is loving her new job.

For more information and practice, see page 156.

6 Complete the table with these stative verbs. Can you add more?

belong	contain	know	love	mean
need	sound	suppose	taste	understand

Categories	Stative verbs
thoughts / mental processes	believe, _____ , _____ , _____ , _____
the senses	hear, _____ , _____
emotions	want, _____ , _____
possession	have, _____ , _____

7 Complete the sentences with the simple present or present continuous forms of the verbs. Are they stative or dynamic?

1 a I _____ (think) this color is OK.
  b We _____ (think) about moving.
2 a The Quechua people _____ (come) from South America.
  b A lot of people _____ (come) to the city to live these days.
3 a I _____ (love) purple flowers.
  b My sister is on vacation in Peru. She _____ (love) it!

Vocabulary time expressions

8 Find these time expressions in the article and in the comments in Exercise 5. Then complete the table with the expressions and add more.

always	at the moment	often	this fall
today	usually		

Simple present	Present continuous
on weekends	right now
every day	this month
never	this week
_____	_____
_____	_____

9 Write questions with these verbs using the simple present or present continuous and time expressions. Then work in pairs. Ask and answer your questions.

buy	dress	eat	try out	wear	work

Do you usually dress differently on weekends?

Not really, no.

Speaking

10 Work in pairs. Ask and answer the questions like the ones below about these activities. Find three things you have in common.

cook a meal
decorate your house
do housework
dress up
go online
go out with friends
go shopping
go to evening classes
go to an exercise class
learn a new skill
make something with your hands
read a new book
spend time with your family

How often do you cook a meal?

Are you cooking a meal at the moment?

When do you usually cook meals?

What are you cooking these days?

1b Culture and color

Vocabulary feelings and personal states

1 Work in pairs. Which color do you associate with the words *love* and *anger*?

2 Choose the correct word for each definition. Check that you understand the meaning of the other words. Use a dictionary if necessary.

1 *passion / prosperity* financial success
2 *love / luck* what happens by chance
3 *courage / anger* the ability to face dangerous situations without being afraid
4 *happiness / wisdom* the ability to make good decisions based on experience
5 *knowledge / sorrow* information you get from experience or education
6 *power / sadness* unhappiness
7 *joy / mourning* great sadness when someone dies
8 *pride / envy* wanting what someone else has

Listening

3 🔊 **1** Work in pairs. Take the quiz *Colors and their meaning*. Then listen and check your answers.

4 🔊 **1** Listen again and complete the notes.

Color	Place	Meaning
red	Western cultures	love, passion, [1] ....
	Eastern cultures	luck, prosperity, courage
yellow	China India	power wisdom, [2] ....
orange	Japan	happiness, [3] ....
[4]	international Western cultures	environmentalism envy

5 Do these colors mean the same in your culture?

Colors and their meaning

1 Look at the photo. Where are the women going?
a to a birthday party
b to a wedding

2 Does red have different meanings in Eastern and Western cultures?
a yes   b no

3 Where does yellow symbolize wisdom?
a China   b India

4 Which color means "happiness" in Japan?
a orange   b pink

5 Who uses green as their symbol?
a the environmental movement
b paint manufacturers

6 Pronunciation questions

a  🔊 2 Listen to the questions and repeat them. Notice how the speaker's voice rises at the end of questions that begin with verbs, and rises then falls for questions that begin with *Wh-* words.

1 Do you want to do this quiz?

2 Where are the women going?

b 🔊 3 Listen and repeat these questions.

1 Where does yellow symbolize wisdom?
2 Is it China?
3 What's the next question?
4 Are there any more questions?
5 Do you want to give it a try?

Grammar question forms

7 Match the questions in the quiz with these statements (a–c).

a We use *do* and *does* to make questions in the simple present.

b When we make questions with *be* or modal verbs (like *can*), we invert the subject and the verb.

c When the question word is the subject of the question, we don't invert the subject and the verb.

▶ QUESTION FORMS

(why / where /	are can	you you	find	happy? this word?
how / what etc.)	does is	it she	work ? doing?	
		who / what	uses	this color?

For more information and practice, see page 156.

8 Look at the grammar box. Complete the *blue* and *yellow* quiz questions with verbs or question words.

9 Work in two pairs in groups of four.

Pair A: Turn to page 153 and follow the instructions.

Pair B: Turn to page 154 and follow the instructions.

Quiz

1 Where _____ the Tuareg—or "blue people" —originally come from?

2 _____ lives in the Blue House in South Korea?

3 What _____ the name of the country where the Blue Nile begins?

4 Which part of the US _____ famous for "the blues" (music)?

The color blue

The color yellow

1 Which fruit _____ the California Yellow Fruit Festival celebrate?

2 _____ sport gives a yellow jersey to the winner?

3 Where _____ yellow taxi cabs come from originally?

4 Where _____ you see the house that inspired Van Gogh's *Yellow House* painting?

Writing and speaking

10 You are going to learn about your classmates. First, prepare some questions. Match questions 1–4 with the follow-up questions (a–d). Then write four more follow-up questions of your own for questions 5–8.

1 What do you do?
2 Do you live near here?
3 Are you from a large family?
4 How many languages do you speak?
5 Why are you learning English?
6 What do you think of the course?
7 Are you taking any other classes at the moment?
8 Do you have any hobbies?

a How well do you speak _____ ?
b How many _____ do you have?
c Can you walk home from here?
d Do you enjoy your job?

11 Now use your questions to learn about three or four classmates. Be prepared to share what you learn with the class.

1c Red is for winners

Reading

1 How many sports teams can you write down in one minute? What are their team colors? Which are the most successful?

2 Work in pairs. Read the article headline on page 15 and discuss what you think it means. Choose one of these options (a–c).

   a Traditional gold medals are now red.
   b Teams with the word "red" in their names win more often.
   c Red sports clothes lead to more success.

3 Read the article quickly. Check your ideas from Exercise 2.

4 Find information about these people in the article and correct the factual mistakes in these sentences.

   1 Russell Hill and Robert Barton are athletes.
   2 Joanna Setchell studies African birds.
   3 Jonathan Blount is an anthropologist.

5 Match the research topics (1–4) with the scientists' conclusions (a–d).

   1 Results at the Olympic Games
   2 African mandrills' success with the opposite sex
   3 Male and female zebra finches
   4 The color of birds' beaks

   a The color red gives some male monkeys an advantage.
   b The color red makes some male birds more successful.
   c Brightly colored beaks are indicators of healthier birds.
   d The color red can give some athletes an advantage.

Critical thinking conclusions

6 Read Hill and Barton's conclusion carefully. Which statement (a–c) means the same thing?

> When sports competitors are equally matched, the team dressed in red is more likely to win, according to a new study.

   a The color red can make a weak athlete successful against a strong athlete.
   b The color red is only an important factor when there is very little difference in the athletes' skill.
   c The color red does not affect results when there is very little difference in the athletes' skill.

Vocabulary and speaking the roles we play

7 Look at the list of roles people can have. Which of these roles are mentioned in the text?

anthropologist	athlete	biologist	colleague
competitor	contestant	friend	manager
mentor	opponent	parent	primatologist
researcher	scientist	teacher	

> ▶ **WORDBUILDING activity → person**
> We can change the ending of some nouns to make words that describe what people do.
> anthropology → anthropologist
> win → winner

8 Work in pairs. Take turns choosing one of the words and describing what a person in that role does. Your partner will guess the word.

> *This person helps you at work, but is not your boss.*

> *colleague*

9 How many different roles do you play in your life? Compare with your partner.

> *Well, I'm participating in a photography competition, so I suppose I'm a competitor.*

When sports competitors are equally matched, the team dressed in red is more likely to win, according to a new study.

That is the conclusion of anthropologists Russell Hill and Robert Barton, after studying the results of one-on-one boxing, tae kwon do, Greco-Roman wrestling, and freestyle wrestling matches at the Olympic Games. Their study shows that when a competitor is equally matched with an opponent in fitness and skill, the athlete wearing red is more likely to win.

Hill and Barton report that when one contestant is much better than the other, color has no effect on the result. However, when there is only a small difference between them, the effect of color is sufficient to tip the scale. The anthropologists say that the number of times red wins is not simply by chance, but is statistically significant.

Joanna Setchell, a primate researcher, has found similar results in nature. She studies the large African monkeys known as mandrills. Mandrills have bright red noses that stand out against their white faces. Setchell's work shows that the dominant males—the ones who are more successful with females—have a brighter red nose than other males. Setchell says that the finding that red also has an advantage in human athletics does not surprise her, and she adds that "the idea of the study is very clever."

Hill and Barton got the idea for their research because of the role that the color red plays in the animal world. "Red seems to be the color, across species, that signals male dominance," Barton says. They thought that "there might be a similar effect in humans." Setchell, the primatologist, agrees: "As Hill and Barton say, humans redden when we are angry and go pale when we're scared. These are very important signals to other individuals."

> **Red seems to be the color... that signals male dominance.**

In a study demonstrating the effect of red among birds, scientists put red plastic rings on the legs of male zebra finches and found an increase in the birds' success with female zebra finches. Zebra finches already have bright red beaks, so this study suggests that, as with Olympic athletes, an extra flash of red is significant. In fact, researchers from the University of Glasgow say that the birds' brightly colored beaks are an indicator of health. Jonathan Blount, a biologist, says that females of many species choose to mate with the brightest males. Blount and his colleagues think that bright red or orange beaks attract females because they mean that the males are healthier. Nothing in nature is simple, however, because in species such as the blue-footed booby, a completely different color seems to give the male birds the same advantage with females.

> **... bright red or orange beaks attract females because they mean that the males are healthier.**

Meanwhile, what about those athletes who win in their events while wearing red? Do their clothes give them an unintentional advantage? Maybe it's time for new regulations on team colors?

Team color red

The toucan is one of many birds with a brightly colored beak.

The blue-footed booby's feet are the main attraction.

fitness (n) /ˈfɪtnɪs/ health and strength
indicator (n) /ˈɪndɪˌkeɪtər/ sign
regulations (n) /ˌregyəˈleɪʃənz/ rules
significant (adj) /sɪgˈnɪfɪkənt/ 1 not by chance
  2 with an important meaning
unintentional (adj) /ˌʌnɪnˈtenʃən(ə)l/ not planned

1d First impressions

Real life opening and closing conversations

You never get a second chance to make a good first impression.

- ☐ Dress appropriately. A dark blue suit is great for a business meeting, a red tie or scarf suggests power and energy. But what if you work in the arts?
- ☐ Be punctual, courteous, and positive.
- ☐ Make sure you know the other person's name. Use it!
- ☐ Make the other person the focus of your attention. Sound interested! Ask questions!
- ☐ Know what you want to say and say it effectively!
- ☐ Don't forget to follow up on your meeting with a phone call or an email.

1 Work in groups. Discuss the text above with respect to your own country.

    1 Do the colors and clothes mean the same thing?
    2 What does *punctual* mean?
    3 Do you use first or last names?
    4 Which advice is appropriate in your country?
    5 Which advice is not appropriate in your country?

2 🔊 4 Listen to four participants at a business skills seminar. They are role-playing "first meetings." Mark the points on the handout above that the speakers follow.

3 🔊 4 Look at the expressions for opening and closing conversations. Listen again and mark the expressions you hear. Which pair of participants do you think gave the best performance?

> ▶ **OPENING AND CLOSING CONVERSATIONS**
>
> **Opening a conversation**
> May I introduce myself?
> Allow me to introduce myself.
> Hi, how are you? I'm…
> It's a pleasure to meet you.
> Nice meeting you.
>
> **Closing a conversation and moving on**
> Thanks for your time.
> It's been good talking to you.
> Let me give you my card.
> Let's stay in touch.
> Why don't I give you my card?
> How about meeting again?

4 Pronunciation short questions

a 🔊 5 Listen to these exchanges. Notice how the speakers use short questions to show interest.

    1 —I mostly work on web advertising.
      —Do you?

    2 —I'm in sales.
      —Oh, are you?

    3 —Oh yes, my brother goes to your gym.
      —Does he?

b Work in pairs. Practice the exchanges.

5 Look at the audioscript on page 173. Practice the conversations with your partner.

6 Imagine you are a participant at a business skills seminar. Complete the profile information card and then do the seminar task. Use the expressions for opening and closing conversations to help you.

> Name _____
> Company _____
>
> Position _____
>
> Responsibilities _____
>
> Current projects you are involved in _____

> **First Impressions**
> Task: You are at a networking event. Introduce yourself to as many people as you can and arrange to follow up useful contacts. You only have two minutes with each person.

networking [n] /ˈnetˌwɜrkɪŋ/ *making useful business contacts*

7 Work in pairs. Compare the information you found out about different people in Exercise 6.

1e About us

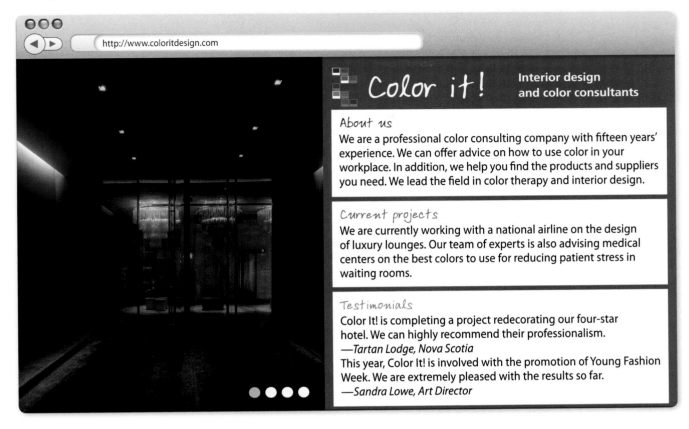

http://www.coloritdesign.com

Color it!
Interior design and color consultants

About us
We are a professional color consulting company with fifteen years' experience. We can offer advice on how to use color in your workplace. In addition, we help you find the products and suppliers you need. We lead the field in color therapy and interior design.

Current projects
We are currently working with a national airline on the design of luxury lounges. Our team of experts is also advising medical centers on the best colors to use for reducing patient stress in waiting rooms.

Testimonials
Color It! is completing a project redecorating our four-star hotel. We can highly recommend their professionalism.
—*Tartan Lodge, Nova Scotia*
This year, Color It! is involved with the promotion of Young Fashion Week. We are extremely pleased with the results so far.
—*Sandra Lowe, Art Director*

Writing a website profile

1 Read the information about the Color It! consulting company. Who (a–d) do you think would be interested in their services?

   a   a nursery school with a new location
   b   a newlywed couple buying their first home
   c   a paint manufacturer
   d   a fashion store opening new branches

2 **Writing skill criteria for writing**

a Read the information again. Choose the correct option.

   1   text type: *website / letter*
   2   style: *neutral / formal / informal*
   3   reader: *current clients / potential clients*
   4   purpose: *to promote the company / to advertise a product*

b Which features of the text helped you decide your answers in Exercise 2a?

3 Underline these expressions and verbs in the text.

   1   time expressions
   2   expressions that signal additional information
   3   verbs describing the company's work

4 Complete the sentences with some of the expressions you underlined in Exercise 3.

   1   We are _____ carrying out market research into cell phone use for a large telecommunications company. _____ , we are advising a fast food company on a new logo.
   2   _____ our company is opening four new offices in major cities in the US. We are _____ expanding to Latin America.

5 Work in groups. Imagine you run a small business together. Decide on your company name, field of work, and some current projects.

6 Work on your own. Write a website profile to promote your business. Use the Color It! profile and the categories in Exercise 2 to help you.

7 Work in your groups again. Read your profiles and choose the one that best promotes your company. The best profile should have no spelling mistakes and should make readers understand exactly what your company does.

Peruvian weavers

These villagers are part of something new.

Before you watch

1 Work in groups. Look at the photo and discuss these questions.

   1 Where do the people come from?
   2 What are they doing?

2 Complete the summary with these words.

> business   cooked   farming   self-sufficient
> shawls   traditions   village   visitors   weavers

The video is about a group of women [1]_____ in a small [2]_____ in Peru. Traditionally in this village, women [3]_____, looked after the children, and made cloth, and men farmed. But now [4]_____ is not enough to support a family, and some women have formed a new type of [5]_____ : a weavers' cooperative. The women use traditional methods to weave blankets, [6]_____, and ponchos that they sell to [7]_____ . In this way, they preserve their identity and [8]_____ but also make some money that helps them become [9]_____ .

While you watch

3 Watch the video and check your answers from Exercise 2.

4 Put these statements in the order you hear them.

   a Farming has long been a tradition in Chinchero.
   b Now, in Chinchero, weaving isn't just a tradition. It's a way to make money.
   c A few people from the village… catch the sheep and prepare the knife.
   d I learned when I was in the third grade.
   e The methods they use are traditional, but these villagers are part of something new.
   f They want to keep the Peruvian weaving traditions alive.

5 Answer the questions.

   1 Who is Nilda Cayanupa?

   2 Why did she start the cooperative?

   3 What was her dream?

   4 How did one man get involved in the weaving?

   5 How much money can the women make?

After you watch

6 **Roleplay an interview with Nilda**

Work in pairs.

Student A: You are a journalist for *National Geographic*. Prepare to ask Nilda:

- how the cooperative started.
- what is special about the cooperative.
- what the women have learned to do.
- what the women do with the money they make.
- how life is changing in the village.

Student B: You are Nilda. Look at the ideas above and think about what you are going to say to the journalist.

Act out the interview, then change roles.

7 At the end of the video, the narrator says: "Many threads together are stronger than one alone." How is this true for the women of Chinchero? Do you think this is always true?

8 Work in groups. Ask and answer the questions with other people in your group and write down their answers. Then report the results to the class.

   1 Do you like the clothes the women make?
   2 Have you ever worn traditional clothes? When?
   3 Do your clothes express who you are?
   4 Which is more important to you: brand or color and design?

---

blanket (n) /ˈblæŋkɪt/ a covering that keeps you warm in bed

cloth (n) /klɔθ/ material used for making clothes, etc.

cooperative (n) /koʊˈɑpərətɪv/ a business or organization owned by the people who work in it and who all profit from it

poncho (n) /ˈpɑntʃoʊ/ a traditional South American coat made from a single piece of cloth, with a hole in the middle for the head

self-sufficient (adj) /ˈself səˈfɪʃənt/ able to provide everything you need for yourself

shawl (n) /ʃɔl/ an article of clothing worn around the shoulders

spin (v) /spɪn / twist fibers of a material into thread to make cloth

thread (n) /θred/ a long thin line of fiber

weave (v) /wiv/ make cloth by crossing threads over and under each other

weaver (n) /ˈwivər/ a person who weaves

wool (n) /wʊl/ a material made from the hair of sheep and other animals

yarn (n) /yɑrn/ a long thick line of fiber made by twisting threads together

UNIT 1 REVIEW

Grammar

1 Work in pairs. Discuss the questions.

1 What do you think the life of an Olympic athlete is like?
2 How do athletes prepare for top-level competitions?
3 How do you think it feels to compete in major competitions?

2 Jiao Liuyang is a gold-medal winning swimmer for China. Complete the interview that she gave a reporter.

1 Q: What _____ (this championship / mean) to you?
   A: Actually, I _____ (not / think) too much about it. I _____ (concentrate) on what I _____ (do) now.

2 Q: _____ (what / influence) you during a race?
   A: When you _____ (hear) people cheering your name, it _____ (make) it more exciting.

3 Q: _____ (you / train) every day?
   A: At the moment, I _____ (do) a little more than usual. I only _____ (get) Sundays off.

4 Q: So this competition _____ (affect) your training routine?
   A: Yes, the routine _____ (change) before a major championship. And this time, we _____ (try) different methods for training.

3 Work in pairs. Compare your answers from Exercise 2. Then act out the interview.

I CAN	
ask and answer questions about things that are always and generally true, and routines (simple present)	☐
ask and answer questions about things happening now (present continuous)	☐
talk about possessions and states: thoughts, etc. (stative verbs)	☐

Vocabulary

4 Tell your partner about something you do or are doing at these times. Then choose one activity of your partner's that you don't know very much about and ask follow-up questions.

always	on weekends	every day
never	often	right now
this month	this week	today
usually		

5 Race your partner to figure out what these words for people's roles are by filling in the missing vowels. Do you know people who have these roles? Tell your partner about them.

thlt	cntstnt	prnt
blgst	mngr	rsrchr
cllg	mntr	scntst
cmpttr	ppnnt	tchr

I CAN	
talk about feelings and personal states	☐
use time expressions with the simple present and present continuous	☐
talk about the roles people have	☐

Real life

6 Work in small groups. You are at a reception for a local sports charity. Choose one of the roles from Exercise 5. Then act out conversations with different partners using these pairs of expressions to begin and end the conversation.

1 "May I introduce myself?"
   "Let's stay in touch."
2 "Hi! My name's…"
   "Let me give you my card."
3 "Hi, how are you? I'm…"
   "How about meeting again?"

I CAN	
introduce myself in formal and informal situations	☐
open and close a conversation	☐
ask for and give personal information	☐

Speaking

7 Choose a role: a successful athlete, movie star, politician, etc. Then work in pairs and tell each other who you are.

8 Work on your own. Prepare questions to interview your partner about their success in their career. Use the ideas from Exercise 2. Then take turns asking and answering your questions.

Unit 2 Performance

Mexican dancers

1 Look at the photo of a traditional dance from Mexico. With a partner, discuss: what other types of traditional dances do you know about?

2 Which word is the odd one out in each group? Why?

1 actor audience dance director
dance – all the others are people
2 choreographer conductor musician play
3 concert dancer musical show
4 act comedian entertainer magician
5 band choir orchestra singer
6 ballet clown drama opera
7 blues jazz drummer flamenco
8 dancing acting hiking singing

3 Work in pairs. Are you interested in the arts? Discuss these questions.

1 How often do you go to concerts, shows, or the theater?
2 What are your favorite types of entertainment?
3 What traditional events in your country or region do you enjoy?
4 Do you like taking part in performances or do you prefer being in the audience?

2a A world of music

Vocabulary musical styles

1 What kind of music do you like? Write a list of as many types of music as you can in two minutes. Then work in pairs and discuss your lists. Use the expressions below to help you. Do you have similar tastes?

> *What do you think of rap?*
>
> *I hate it. It's so repetitive.*

I love/hate/enjoy/adore it.
I'm (not) into it.
I can't stand it.
I kind of like / don't mind it.

2 Work in pairs. Match the music genres (1–8) with their countries of origin (a–h). Check your answers with your instructor.

1 blues	a Jamaica
2 bossa nova	b Cuba
3 charanga	c US
4 fado	d Brazil
5 flamenco	e Mongolia
6 hoomii	f Spain
7 reggae	g Portugal
8 taiko drumming	h Japan

3 Work in pairs. Describe as many of the music genres in Exercise 2 as you know. Use these words.

catchy   cheerful   lively   melancholy
melodic   moving   repetitive   rhythmic
tuneless   unusual

Listening

4 🔊 **6** Listen to a radio show about world fusion music. Complete the sentences.

1 World fusion mixes several different
  ....
2 Manu Chao sings in .... languages.
3 Paul Simon has worked with .... artists Ladysmith Black Mambazo.
4 Peter Gabriel is a .... musician.
5 Youssou N'Dour is a Senegalese ....
6 Zap Mama are a world fusion group from ....

While waiting for their meal to cook, a group in Darhan, Mongolia, enjoys a song.

Photograph by Christopher De Bruyn

5 🔊 **6** Listen again. Correct the factual errors in the sentences.

1 Manu Chao has not been successful in the French-speaking world.
2 World fusion has become better-known since the release of Paul Simon's film *Graceland*.
3 Peter Gabriel has been part of WOMAD for two years.
4 Zap Mama have had several hits in Belgium.

6 Work in pairs. What did you learn from the radio show?

Grammar present perfect

7 Look at the sentences in Exercise 5. Which one of these statements is false?

1 The activities or situations started at some time in the past.
2 The activities or situations continue into the present.
3 The activities or situations ended in the past.
4 We use *since* with the starting point of an activity.
5 We use *for* with a period of time long ended.

8 Look at the grammar box. Complete the sentences with the present perfect form of the verbs. Which verbs are regular? Which are irregular?

1 Manu Chao _____ (live) in France for most of his life.
2 Youssou N'Dour _____ (become) very popular since working with Peter Gabriel.
3 Young musicians _____ (mix) folk with punk.
4 What _____ (happen) to world fusion since the 1980s?
5 We _____ (hear) lots of great music in the past few years.
6 How many albums _____ Zap Mama _____ (make)?

► PRESENT PERFECT		
		past participle
I/you/we/they	have (not)	been
he/she/it	has (not)	had
What	has	happened?

For more information and practice, see page 157.

9 Complete the paragraph with the present perfect form of the verbs.

The number of online music sites **1** _____ (grow) enormously since Internet connections became cheaper. In many ways these sites **2** _____ (take over) the traditional roles of both radio stations and music stores. Buying music online **3** _____ (become) more popular than many music companies imagined: you can now download music files directly to your music player. It **4** _____ (also / get) much easier to listen to different kinds of music on blogs and sites. Artists **5** _____ (start) uploading their music directly to the Internet and some **6** _____ (find) mainstream success that way.

10 Are these expressions used with *for* or *since*? Write two lists.

a couple of days	1986	a while
a few months	ages	centuries
I was a child	July	last Monday
my last vacation	lunchtime	some time
the day before yesterday	years	

11 Write the present perfect form of the verbs. Then complete the sentences so that they are true for you. Work in pairs and compare your sentences.

1 I _____ (live) here for _____ .
2 I _____ (be) at my current job since _____ .
3 I _____ (know) my best friend since _____ .
4 I _____ (not / listen to) _____ for ages.
5 I _____ (always / want) to _____ .
6 I _____ (never / have) _____ .
7 I _____ (study) English since _____ .
8 I _____ (be) in this class for _____ .

► ALREADY, JUST, and YET
They've already had several international hits.
You've just heard a [...] track from Manu Chao's latest album.
He hasn't had a big impact in this country yet.

For more information, see page 158.

12 Match the comments (1–4) with the responses (a–d). Complete the sentences with *already, just,* and *yet*. Check your answers with your instructor.

1 Have you heard Shakira's new single?
2 Do you want to borrow this DVD of Matt Damon's latest movie?
3 Have you seen *Gone with the Wind* _____ ?
4 The National Ballet has _____ announced its new season.

a No, thanks. I've _____ seen it.
b Yes, we have. It's even better than the book.
c They have? Which ballets are they doing?
d No, not _____ . Is it as good as her last one?

Speaking

13 Work in pairs. Act out conversations like the ones in Exercise 12. Use these words.

a new album / song / band
a musical / show / play / concert / movie
an exhibit / a festival

The new Arctic Monkeys album has just come out. Have you heard it?

No, I haven't. What's it like?

2b Dance across America

Reading

1 Work in pairs. Answer the questions.

1 What kind of dances are traditional in your country?
2 Have you ever been to a dance class or learned a dance?
3 Do you dance at special occasions? Which ones?
4 How does dancing make you feel?

2 Read the article *Dance across America*. What is the article about? Choose the correct option (a–c).

a professional dancers
b ordinary people
c professional dancers and ordinary people

3 Underline three reasons why people dance. Circle three effects dancing has on people.

4 The article talks about the role of dancing in people's lives. Can you think of other activities people do to:

1 make them feel young?   *keep in shape*
2 meet people?
3 have a social life?
4 change their mood?

DANCE ACROSS AMERICA

Before there was the written word, there was the language of dance. Dance expresses love and hate, joy and sorrow, life and death, and everything else in between.

Dance in America is everywhere. We dance from Florida to Alaska, and from coast to coast. We dance to celebrate or just to fill the time.

"I adore dancing," says Lester Bridges, the owner of a dance studio in Iowa. "I can't imagine doing anything else with my life." Bridges runs dance classes for all ages. "Teaching dance is wonderful. My older students say it makes them feel young. It's marvelous to watch them. For many of them, it's a way of meeting people and having a social life."

So why do we dance? "I can tell you about one young couple," says Bridges. "They're learning to do traditional dances. They arrive at the class in a bad mood and they leave with a smile. Dancing seems to change their mood completely."

So, do we dance to make ourselves feel better, calmer, healthier? Andrea Hillier, a choreographer, says "Dance, like the rhythm of a beating heart, is life. Even after all these years, I want to get better and better. I keep practicing even when I'm exhausted. I find it hard to stop! Dancing reminds me I'm alive."

Grammar verb patterns: *-ing* form and *to* + infinitive

5 Look at the grammar box. Choose the correct option in these sentences.

1 We use the *-ing* form of the verb after certain verbs, as the subject of a sentence and after *adjectives / prepositions*.

2 We use the infinitive of the verb (*to* + base form) after certain verbs and after *adjectives / prepositions*.

▶ VERB PATTERNS: *-ING* FORM AND INFINITIVE			
-ing form	I/you/we/they/he/she	adore(s)	dancing.
	It's a way	of	meeting people.
	Dancing	is	wonderful.
infinitive	I/you/we/they/he/she	want(s)	to get better.
	It's	marvelous	to watch.

For more information and practice, see page 158.

6 In the article, underline examples of the patterns above. Then complete the lists with the verbs in the article.

1 verb + *-ing* form: adore, _____ , _____
2 verb + infinitive: learn, _____ , _____

7 Each option in these sentences is grammatically possible. Which one is not logically possible?

1 Andrea Hillier *agrees / expects / intends* to get better.
2 Some students *need / hope / pretend* to make new friends.
3 One student *involves / keeps / practices* doing the steps every day.
4 All our best students *choose / promise / refuse* to practice regularly.
5 Few students *decide / help / plan* to give up.

8 Complete the sentences with the *-ing* form and infinitive form of the verbs. Which sentences are true about you? Which do you agree with? Then work in pairs. Tell your partner.

1 I enjoy _____ (do) creative activities.
2 _____ (paint) is one of my favorite hobbies.
3 It's hard _____ (be) completely original.
4 I often imagine _____ (change) my lifestyle.
5 I'm too old _____ (learn) something new.
6 I'm learning _____ (play) the piano.
7 I'm thinking about _____ (try) folk dancing.
8 I never seem _____ (find) time to meet people.

Vocabulary emotions

9 What kind of things can change your mood? Match the two parts of the sentences.

1 Going out dancing
2 Every time I hear a sad song, I want
3 That music is so cheerful—it always
4 It's a really funny movie. I can't stop
5 Seeing horror movies makes me

a feel scared.
b laughing when I think about it.
c makes me smile.
d really energizes me up.
e to cry.

10 Think of specific examples for each sentence in Exercise 9. Then work in pairs. Tell your partner about them.

> *I don't go out dancing every week, maybe a couple of times a month. I always have a good time. It puts me in a good mood.*

Speaking

11 Use these phrases or your own ideas to make sentences that are true for you. Write sentences with the *-ing* form and the infinitive form of the verbs.

act	perform in public
be behind the scenes	play an instrument
be in the spotlight	sing
be on stage	tell jokes
go to dances	give a speech

1 I really enjoy _____
2 I can't imagine _____
3 I hate _____
4 _____ makes me feel great.
5 It's not easy _____
6 I'm learning _____

12 Work in pairs. Compare your sentences from Exercise 11 and find things you feel the same way about. Ask follow-up questions.

> *So, you enjoy performing in public. What kind of performances do you do?*

> *Well, I like singing karaoke at parties! And it makes my friends laugh!*

2c A world together

Reading

1 Work in groups. What does the term *globalization* mean to your group? Give examples.

2 Read the first two paragraphs of the article. Compare your answer from Exercise 1 with the information.

3 Read the rest of the article. Which paragraph talks about:

1 American products in other countries?
2 globalization in the future?
3 the speed of the globalization process?

4 What examples of globalization does the author give for these things?

1 dance
2 food
3 dolls
4 the English language
5 American TV shows

5 Which of these statements (a–d) agree with the article?

a It's hard to find examples of globalization in everyday life.
b Globalization is not a new phenomenon, but the speed of change these days is new.
c Some people think that globalization is a negative thing.
d The author thinks that world cultures cannot resist Western influences.

Critical thinking sources

6 Find these phrases in the article. Why does the author put some words in quotation marks? Match the phrases (1–4) with the reasons (a–b).

1 These are "globalization" moments. (paragraph 2)
2 …"is a reality, not a choice." (paragraph 3)
3 …one big "McWorld." (paragraph 3)
4 "We've taken an American box,"… (paragraph 4)

a The author is reporting someone else's actual words.
b The author wants to emphasize an idea.

7 Which statement best reflects the text? Choose one option (a–c).

a The author thinks globalization is a good thing.
b The author thinks globalization is a bad thing.
c The author does not express her opinion about globalization.

8 What is your opinion? Is globalization a good or a bad thing? Tell your group.

Vocabulary global culture

> ▶ **WORDBUILDING adjective + noun**
> Some adjectives and nouns often go together.
> *outside world   popular culture*

9 Complete the sentences with these words from the article.

connections	culture	influences	market	world

1 Television is a good example of **popular** _____ .
2 There's a **growing** _____ for reality TV.
3 We're trying to encourage **cultural** _____ between our two countries.
4 Many societies have been open to **Western** _____ .
5 Do they have any contact with the **outside** _____ ?

Speaking

10 Work in pairs. Make notes about how things have changed since the year 2000. Use some of these ideas and ideas of your own.

- Popular culture: reality TV, social networking, international movies and music
- Technology: digital photography, phone technology, the Internet
- The economy and work: where things are made, working abroad

11 Work in groups. Compare your ideas and discuss how things have changed in your area or country. Decide which are the biggest changes at the local and national level. Then present your conclusions to the class.

Digital photography has become much more popular.

Yes, a lot of people use digital cameras these days.

A world together

Goods move. People move. Ideas move. And cultures change.

BY ERLA ZWINGLE

Once I start looking for them, I realize these moments are everywhere. One day, I'm sitting in a coffee shop in London having a cup of Italian espresso served by an Algerian waiter, listening to the Beach Boys playing in the background. Another day, I'm eating in a restaurant in New Delhi that serves Lebanese food to the music of a Filipino band, in rooms decorated with a vintage poster for a blues concert in New Orleans.

These are "globalization" moments. We are in the middle of a worldwide change in cultures—a transformation of entertainment, business, and politics. Popular culture has crossed borders in ways we have never seen before. According to social scientists, our world is shrinking. In Japan, people have become flamenco fanatics and there are hundreds of dance schools around the country. In the last few years, dozens of top Spanish flamenco artists have given performances there. It's a huge and growing market. Meanwhile, in Denmark people have discovered a new interest in Italian food, and pasta imports have grown 500% over the last decade. And the classic American blonde Barbie doll now comes in about 30 national varieties, including Austrian and Moroccan.

How do people feel about globalization? It depends to a large extent on where they live and how much money they have. However, globalization, as one report has stated, "is a reality, not a choice." Humans have always developed commercial and cultural connections, but these days computers, the Internet, cell phones, cable TV, and cheaper air transportation have accelerated and complicated these connections. Nevertheless, the basic dynamic is the same:

Goods move. People move. Ideas move. And cultures change. The difference now is the speed and extent of these changes. Television had 50 million users after thirteen years; the Internet had the same number after only five years. But now that more than one-fifth of all the people in the world speak at least some English, critics of globalization say that we are one big "McWorld."

But I have discovered that cultures are as resourceful, resilient, and unpredictable as the people they include. In Los Angeles, I saw more diversity than I thought possible at Hollywood High School, where the student body speaks 32 different languages. In Shanghai, I found that the television show *Sesame Street* has been redesigned by Chinese educators to teach Chinese values and traditions. "We've taken an American box," one told me, "and put Chinese content into it." In India, where there are more than 400 languages and several very strict religions, McDonald's serves lamb instead of beef and offers a vegetarian menu acceptable to even the most orthodox Hindu.

So what's next? It's the eve of the millennium and the remote Himalayan country of Bhutan has just granted its citizens access to television—the last country on the planet to do so. The outside world has suddenly appeared in stores and living rooms across the country. What will happen now—when an isolated and deeply conservative society is exposed to hip-hop and MTV?

eve (n) /iv/ the night before a significant date or day
vintage (adj) /ˈvɪntɪdʒ/ from an earlier time or era

2d What's playing?

Real life choosing an event

1 Work in pairs. Look at the ads. Which event appeals to you the most—and the least?

2 🎧 **7** Read the comments. Then listen to the conversation and write the number of the ad (1–3) next to the comments. Which event do they decide to go and see?

1 It sounds really awful.
2 That sounds really interesting.
3 Apparently, it's absolutely superb.
4 It looks pretty good.
5 Jackie Chan is absolutely hilarious.
6 He's not very funny.

3 🎧 **7** Look at the expressions for choosing an event. Listen again and mark the expressions Lesley and Richard use.

> ▶ **CHOOSING AN EVENT**
>
> **Suggestions and responses**
> Do you feel like going out tonight?
> Do you want to go to the movies?
> Would you like to see a movie?
> Do you like the sound of that?
>
> Sure, why not?
> Yeah, sure.
> I like the sound of that.
> I'm not crazy about him.
> I'm not in the mood for anything depressing.
> It doesn't really appeal to me.
> It sounds great.
>
> **Details of the event**
> What's playing?
> Who's in it?
> What else is playing?
> Who's it by?
> Where / When / What time is it at?
> What's it about?

Vocabulary describing performances

4 Look at the sentences in Exercise 2. Write the words used before these adjectives. Which adjectives have stronger meanings?

1 _____ _____ : awful, superb, hilarious
2 _____ , _____ , _____ : interesting, good, funny

5 Which words (absolutely, pretty, really, very) do you use with each group of adjectives?

> **A** fantastic   fascinating   spectacular
> terrible   terrific   thrilling   unforgettable

> **B** boring   depressing   disappointing   dull
> entertaining

6 Pronunciation intonation with *really*, *absolutely*, *pretty*, and *very*

a 🎧 **8** Listen to these sentences from Exercise 2 again. Notice how the speakers stress both the adverb and adjective in the affirmative statements.

b Work in pairs. Practice these exchanges paying attention to your intonation.

1 A: What was the movie like?
   B: It was really awful.

2 A: Do you like flamenco?
   B: Yes, I think it's pretty interesting.

3 A: Was it a good festival?
   B: Yes, it was absolutely superb.

4 A: How was the show?
   B: Oh, very entertaining!

7 Work in pairs. Invite your partner to see the event that most appealed to you in Exercise 1. Include words from Exercises 4 and 5. Use the expressions for choosing an event to help you.

2e A portrait of an artist

Writing a profile

1 Work in pairs. Who is your favorite performer or artist? Tell your partner about this person and why you like him/her.

2 Read the portrait of Baz Luhrmann. What kind of information about him does it include? Choose the correct options (a–d).

a his influences c his private life
b his plans d his work

3 Read the profile again. Underline the information that is factual and circle the opinions. Then find two direct quotes from Luhrmann.

4 Which of these adjectives describe the profile? Explain your choice(s).

| balanced | biased | informative |
| objective | personal | subjective |

Baz Luhrmann is a director whose movies include *Strictly Ballroom*, *Romeo+Juliet*, *Moulin Rouge!*, and *Australia*. I have seen every one of his movies and in my opinion, his work just gets better and better. He says that "putting on a show" has always come naturally to him and that Bollywood is his biggest influence. Although he is best known as a film director, Luhrmann has also directed opera. As a result, his movies are usually vibrant, energetic, and spectacular. They have had box office success despite being unusual: in *Romeo+Juliet*, the actors speak in verse, and in *Moulin Rouge!*, they sing their lines. On the other hand, the epic *Australia* didn't go over so well with the critics. Nevertheless, as an ordinary movie fan, I thought it was absolutely fantastic. Luhrmann says the high point of his career has been "achieving so many of the dreams I had as a kid— from going to the Oscars to getting a letter from Marlon Brando." To me, his films have the power of dreams. They take you into thrilling, unforgettable worlds.

5 Writing skill linking ideas (1)

a Look at the table. Which group of words can replace each highlighted word in the profile? Write the words from the profile in the table.

in spite of	even though while	in contrast but however	because of this for that reason so therefore

b Look at the words in bold in the sentences. With which word does the verb form change? When do we use a comma?

1 **Although he is** best-known as a film director, Luhrmann has also directed opera.
2 **Despite being** best known as a film director, Luhrmann has also directed opera.
3 He is best known as a film director. **However**, Luhrmann has also directed opera.

c Rewrite the sentences using the words in parentheses. Make any necessary changes to verbs and punctuation.

1 They have had box office success despite being unusual movies. (even though)
2 I enjoyed *Romeo+Juliet* in spite of not understanding all the dialogue. (but)
3 While I love epic movies, I didn't enjoy this one. (Nevertheless)
4 Although they praised Luhrmann's earlier movies, the critics did not like *Australia*. (In spite of)
5 I've seen all of the movies, but I haven't seen any of the operas. (however)
6 His last movie was absolutely superb. Because of this, I'm looking forward to seeing the next one. (so)

6 Write a profile of an artist whose work you know and enjoy. Make notes under each heading, then write about 150 words. Use a variety of adjectives and linking words.

- Basic biographical information
- Facts (life, work)
- Opinions (mine, others')

7 Use these questions to check your profile.

- Have you used linking words correctly?
- Have you expressed clearly why you like this person's work?

8 Read some of your classmates' profiles and discuss:

- What do you learn about the person from reading the profile?
- Do you agree with the opinions expressed in the profile?

"You hit this point where you're just completely free."

Before you watch

1 Work in groups. Look at the photo and discuss the questions.

    1   What is the man in the photo doing?
    2   How do you think he feels?
    3   What do you think the caption means?

2 Which of these things do you think you will see in this video?

audience	dance	drum	drummer	drumstick
guitar	piano	rock group	theater	

While you watch

3 Check your answers from Exercise 2.

4 Answer the questions.

    1   What is taiko?

    2   Where does it come from?

    3   What has been added recently to traditional taiko?

    4   What three things does taiko bring together?

    5   What effect do pain and fatigue have on some taiko drummers?

5 Make notes about the history of taiko.

2,000 years ago	
The early 1900s	
The mid-1900s	
1968	
Now	

6 Complete the information about Grand Master Seiichi Tanaka and taiko. Then watch the video again and check your answers.

Seiichi Tanaka traveled by [1]_____ from Japan to [2]_____ in the late 60s. When he arrived, he started playing [3]_____ with other people. In the following years, he taught people how to play taiko. Taiko drumming soon became popular. In the 1960s there were only a dozen or so taiko groups, but now there are over [4]_____ in the United States and [5]_____. Master Tanaka believes that energy from nature flows through the [6]_____ of the drummer to the [7]_____ and into the drum.

After you watch

7 **Roleplay finding out about taiko drumming**

Work in pairs.

Student A: You want to join a taiko drum group. Use the ideas below to prepare questions to ask a taiko master.

Student B: You are a master in taiko drumming. Use the ideas below to prepare what you are going to tell someone who wants to join a taiko drum group.

- where it comes from
- what you have to wear
- how fit you have to be
- what you need to buy
- how long it takes to learn

Act out the conversation. Then change roles and act out the conversation again.

8 Work in groups. Discuss the questions.

    1   Have you ever played a musical instrument? Which instrument? When?
    2   Are there any traditional instruments in your country? What are they?
    3   Do you think it is important to maintain traditional forms of music and dance?

---

audience (n) /ˈɔdiəns/ a group of people who watch or listen to something
beat (n) /bit/ rhythm
beat (v) /bit/ hit again and again
boundary (n) /ˈbaʊndri/ limit
community (n) /kəˈmyunɪti/ a group of people who live in an area
drain (v) /dreɪn/ take away from
bring together (v) /ˈbrɪŋ təˈgeðər/ join
drum (n) /drʌm/ a musical instrument that you hit with a stick
drum (v) /drʌm/ play a drum

drummer (n) /ˈdrʌmər/ a person who plays a drum
drumstick (n) /ˈdrʌmˌstɪk/ the stick a drummer uses to hit the drum
essence (n) /ˈesəns/ the most important aspect of something
fear (v) /fɪər/ be afraid of
performance (n) /pərˈfɔrməns/ the act of playing music for other people
pioneer (n) /ˌpaɪəˈnɪər/ one of the first people to do something
unity (n) /ˈyunəti/ the feeling of being together
warrior (n) /ˈwɔriər/ a soldier

UNIT 2 REVIEW

Grammar

1 Work in pairs. Look at the photo and discuss the questions.

1 Are the people spectators or performers?
2 What time of year do you think it is?
3 Where do you think this festival is?

I've lived in Japan ¹_____ three months now and I'm really enjoying it. I ²_____ learned some Japanese, including the word *matsuri*, which means "festival." One of my favorite pastimes is ³_____ to matsuri. I've ⁴_____ returned from the Nango summer jazz festival. It was great ⁵_____ sit in the sunshine and listen to wonderful music! Next is the Tenjin matsuri here in Osaka. It has ⁶_____ part of Osaka's summer events ⁷_____ about a thousand years, and some performances have hardly changed ⁸_____ then—the traditional kagura music, for example. There's also a puppet theater, and we're hoping ⁹_____ join the big procession of boats on the river.

2 Read the blog and check your ideas from Exercise 1.

3 Complete the blog with these missing words. You can use some of the words more than once.

been	for	going	have	just	since	to
yet

4 Tell your partner about a festival you have been to or would like to go to.

I CAN	
talk about things that have happened in a time period up to or including the present	☐
use verb patterns correctly	☐

Vocabulary

5 Work in pairs. Choose the two people who are usually involved in these performances. Then choose four types of performers and tell your partner about people you have heard about.

1 FILM: actor, director, magician
2 CONCERT: clown, conductor, musician
3 BALLET: choreographer, comedian, dancer
4 MUSICAL: photographer, singer, dancer

6 Work in groups. In two minutes, write the names of as many popular art events (movies, plays, exhibitions, performances) as you can. Then discuss the ones you have all heard of using the words in the box. You can't use more than two words to describe one event, but you must continue until everyone has used all the words at least once.

disappointing	depressing	superb	boring
entertaining	fascinating	terrible	dull
unforgettable	spectacular	thrilling	terrific

7 Work in pairs. Describe what kind of music makes you do the following.

cry	feel happy	feel sad	laugh	smile

I CAN	
talk about performers and performances	☐
describe different types of music	☐
give my opinion about art events	☐

Real life

8 Work in pairs. Choose the correct option in the questions. Then take the roles of A and B and act out the conversation, giving answers to the questions and adding more information.

1 A: Do you feel like *to go / going* out tonight?
2 A: Would you like *to see / seeing* a movie?
3 A: *Do you / Would you* like the sound of that?
4 B: Who's *in / on* it?
5 B: Who's it *by / to*?
6 B: What's it *about / of*?

I CAN	
ask for and give information about arts events	☐

Speaking

9 Work in groups. The director Baz Luhrmann says that in his career he has achieved many of the dreams he had as a kid. Which childhood dreams have you already achieved? Which ones have you not achieved yet? Tell your group.

Unit 3 Water

Women in Kenya spend up to five hours a day getting water.
Photograph by Lynn Johnson

1 Work as a class. Look at the photo and answer the questions.

1 Where do you think the women are going?
2 How often do you think they make this trip?
3 What do they do with the water they collect?

2 Work in pairs. Complete the sentences with five of these numbers. Then check your answers with your instructor.

⅕	⅔	3	17	10	46	70	200

1 About _____ percent of the Earth's surface is covered in water.
2 Only _____ percent of the Earth's water is fresh water.
3 Around _____ percent of people don't have running water in their homes.
4 A person in the developing world uses about _____ liters of water each day.
5 In Europe, the average is _____ liters a day.

3 Work in groups. Discuss the questions.

1 Do you know how much water you use every day?
2 Do you try to save water at home? How? Why?

3a Behind the photo

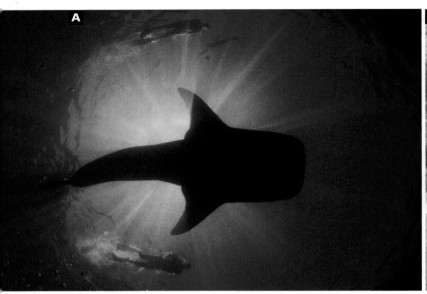

A

B

Vocabulary water and recreation

1 Work in pairs.

Student A: Describe what's happening in one of the photos (A–C). Use words from the boxes.

Student B: Which photo is Student A describing?

Then change roles and repeat.

Activities

diving	fishing	jet-skiing	kayaking
rafting	rowing	sailing	snorkeling
surfing	swimming	water-skiing	windsurfing

Places

lake	marina	ocean	pool	reservoir
river	sea	stream	waterfall	

2 Look at the words in Exercise 1 again. Which do you think are the best places to do the activities?

3 Do you do any of the activities in Exercise 1? Tell your partner.

> *I go fishing about once a month with my brother.*

Listening

4 🎵 **9** Listen to the people in two of the photos talking about their photo. Are the sentences true (T) or false (F)?

1 The girl was rafting down the Zambezi.
2 The raft was approaching some rapids.
3 She saw a hippo near the river bank.
4 The boy learned to dive because he was bored.
5 He went diving in a dangerous cenote.
6 He wasn't concentrating on what he was doing.

5 🎵 **10** What do you think happened next? Choose one of these options (a–c). Then listen to the ending of the story and check your ideas.

1 a The hippo came after them and attacked the raft.
   b A crocodile jumped into the river close to the raft.
   c The raft capsized and they all swam to the river bank.
2 a His air ran out and he had to go to the surface.
   b His mother panicked when she saw a sea snake.
   c He almost got lost in a labyrinth of tunnels.

> ▶ **WORDBUILDING adverbs**
>
> Most adverbs are formed by adding -*ly* to adjectives. Some adverbs and adjectives are the same.
> *quick* (adjective) → *quickly* (adverb)
> *fast* (adjective) = *fast* (adverb)

C

Grammar simple past and past continuous

6 Read these sentences. Underline the simple past verbs and circle the past continuous verbs.

1 We were going around a small island.
2 It jumped into the water.
3 The sun was shining in through an opening in the roof.
4 My mom realized pretty quickly that I was missing and she came after me.

7 Match the sentences (1–4) in Exercise 6 with their meanings (a–d).

a an unfinished activity
b a description
c a finished action
d a sequence of actions in a story

8 Underline the key event in these questions about the rafting story in Exercise 4. Then match the questions (1–2) with the answers (a–b).

1 What were they doing when they saw the hippo?
2 What did they do when they saw the hippo?

a They tried to get away.
b They were coming down the river.

9 Choose the correct option.

1 Questions in the *simple past / past continuous* refer to activities before the key event.
2 Questions in the *simple past / past continuous* refer to activities after the key event.

▶ **SIMPLE PAST and PAST CONTINUOUS**

Simple past
I noticed a big hippo near the river bank.
What did it do?
Past continuous
A crocodile was lying in the sun.
Where was it lying?

For more information and practice, see page 158.

10 Write sentences with the simple past and past continuous. Use *because, when, while,* and *so.*

1 I _____ (take) a photo of the hippo /
I _____ (drop) my camera in the water
2 My friend _____ (fall) out of the raft / he _____ (not / hold) on
3 I _____ (see) some strange fish /
I _____ (dive)
4 I _____ (have) some problems with my mask / my brother _____ (help) me

11 Complete the paragraph about photo A.

When I ¹ _____ (work) in the Maldives, I ² _____ (hear) that there were whale sharks in the area. That's why I ³ _____ (begin) snorkeling—whale sharks are the world's biggest fish! I ⁴ _____ (buy) a cheap snorkel and ⁵ _____ (go) with a group of friends. It was a beautiful day. Almost immediately, a whale shark ⁶ _____ (swim) past the boat. It ⁷ _____ (move) really quickly, but we ⁸ _____ (catch up) with it. We all ⁹ _____ (get) into the water and ¹⁰ _____ (spend) about two minutes with the shark. Afterwards, I ¹¹ _____ (feel) absolutely amazing! It was one of the most fantastic adventures of my life.

Speaking

12 Work in pairs.

Student A: Think about the first time you tried a new skill, or did a hobby or sports activity. Answer your partner's questions without saying what the activity was.

Student B: Ask ten questions and try to find out your partner's activity.

Where were you?

On a boat.

Were you on a lake?

No, the ocean.

Did you have any special equipment?

3b Return to the *Titanic*

Reading

1 Read the interview with the man who discovered the wreck of the *Titanic*. Write the number of the paragraph (1–3) next to the question. There are two extra questions.

a Did you know you were looking at *Titanic* when you saw the first pieces of debris?
b How did the discovery of *Titanic* in 1985 come about?
c How long did it take to locate *Titanic*?
d Tell me about the experience of seeing *Titanic* again in 2004.
e What did you find out about how *Titanic* sank?

2 Read the interview again. Answer the questions.

1 What was the secret mission that Ballard was involved with?
2 How did Ballard and his team feel when they located the *Titanic*?
3 How did Ballard feel when he returned to the wreck in 2004?

3 Do you think the remains of the *Titanic* should be left on the sea bed or should they be put in a museum? Tell your partner.

RETURN *to the* TITANIC

On April 15, 1912, the largest passenger steamship ever built, appropriately named the *Titanic*, sank in the North Atlantic Ocean after hitting an iceberg. The *Titanic* had left Southampton, England, five days earlier and was on her maiden (first) voyage.

In 1985, National Geographic Explorer-in-Residence Dr. Robert Ballard located the wreck of the *Titanic*. He went back to the *Titanic* nineteen years later to see how it had changed.

1 It was the height of the Cold War and in fact I was on a secret mission when we found the *Titanic*. The US Navy had agreed to finance the development of our underwater video technology. In return, we had agreed to use the technology to find two US nuclear submarines that had disappeared in the 1960s.

2 Not at first, because many ships had sunk in that area. When we realized it was the *Titanic*, we jumped for joy. Then we realized we were celebrating at a place where people had died. We actually stopped our work and held a memorial service at that point.

3 I saw champagne bottles, intact, with the corks still in. The box holding the bottles had disappeared long ago. Suddenly, my eye was drawn to a woman's shoe. Nearby I saw a pair of smaller shoes that had perhaps belonged to a child. I felt that the people who had died here in 1912 were speaking to me again. But I knew that a private salvage company had legally removed thousands of objects from the site. A Russian submarine had taken Hollywood filmmaker James Cameron to the wreck. A New York couple had even gotten married on the *Titanic's* bow. It was exactly what I didn't want to happen. I'd asked people to treat the *Titanic's* remains with dignity. Instead, they'd turned her into a freak show. The story of the *Titanic* is not about the ship, it's about the people.

See the whole story on the National Geographic Channel.
Titanic: The Final Secret

bow (n) /baʊ/ the front of a ship or boat
freak show (n) /'frik ˌʃoʊ/ something unusual that people watch for entertainment (often used negatively)
salvage (n) /'sælvɪdʒ/ things recovered from places that have been destroyed in accidents (shipwrecks, fires)

Photograph by Emory Kristof

Grammar past perfect

4 Put each group of events (a–c) in the order they actually took place. Which of these verbs are in the past perfect in the interview? Why?

1. a Ballard found *Titanic*.
   b The US Navy agreed to finance the video technology.
   c Ballard agreed to look for two submarines.
2. a Ballard held a memorial service.
   b Many people died.
   c Ballard celebrated the discovery.
3. a A Russian submarine took James Cameron to the wreck.
   b Ballard noticed a shoe.
   c The box for champagne bottles disappeared.

5 Read these sentences from the interview. Underline what happened first.

1. He went back to the *Titanic* nineteen years later to see how it had changed.
2. Then we realized we were celebrating at a place where people had died.
3. Nearby I saw a pair of smaller shoes that had perhaps belonged to a child.

6 Choose the correct option.

1. We use the past perfect to show that an event took place *before* / *after* other events we have related.
2. When we relate past events in the same order they actually happened, we *have to* / *don't have to* use the past perfect.

> ▶ **PAST PERFECT**
>
> statements: subject + *had (not)* + past participle
> questions: *had* + subject + past participle?
>
> For more information and practice, see page 160.

7 Choose the correct options.

1. When the *Titanic* hit the iceberg, it *was* / *had been* at sea for four days.
2. When it hit the iceberg, it *sank* / *had sunk*.
3. By the time they sounded the ship's alarm, it *was* / *had been* too late.
4. By the time Ballard found the wreck, many items *disappeared* / *had disappeared*.
5. They developed video technology because other techniques *didn't locate* / *hadn't located* the wreck.
6. James Cameron made his movie because he *visited* / *had visited* the wreck.

8 Use the past perfect to answer the questions with your own ideas. Then work in pairs and compare your answers.

1. Why did the *Titanic* collide with an iceberg?
2. Why did so many people die when the ship sank?
3. Why was Dr. Robert Ballard upset in 2004?
4. Why do you think a couple got married at the wreck site?
5. Why do you think James Cameron visited the wreck?

9 Complete the paragraph with the simple past or past perfect form of the verbs.

Captain Henry Morgan [1] _____ (be) one of the most notorious pirates of the 17th century. In 2010, archaeologists [2] _____ (begin) to lift cannons from a ship they [3] _____ (discover) two years earlier, near the coast of Panama. The archaeologists [4] _____ (feel) confident that the ship was Morgan's main ship, *Satisfaction*. This ship and several others [5] _____ (sink) in 1671 when they [6] _____ (hit) rocks. At this time, Morgan [7] _____ (already make) a fortune from his pirate attacks. Three years later he [8] _____ (retire) from pirate activities to become the governor of Jamaica.

Speaking

10 Work in two pairs within a group of four. Read these puzzles.

Pair A: Turn to page 153 and follow the instructions.

Pair B: Turn to page 154 and follow the instructions.

A A ship came across a yacht in the middle of the ocean. There were no other ships or boats in the area. The bodies of several people were floating in the water nearby. What had happened?

B A man was in the middle of the sea in very deep water. He couldn't swim and he wasn't wearing a life jacket. He had been in the water for hours when he finally made it to shore. Why didn't he drown?

3c Love and death in the sea

Reading

1 Work in pairs. Discuss these questions.

1 Do you enjoy swimming?
2 Where do you usually go?
3 Are there any places you would not go swimming? Why not?

2 Enric Sala is a marine ecologist. Read his article on page 39 and answer the questions.

1 What happened to Enric Sala and why?
2 How has the experience changed him?

3 Find these expressions in the article. What do they mean? Choose the correct option.

1 a couple of times
   on *several / two* occasions
2 My guts jump to my throat.
   I feel *afraid / angry*.
3 I decided to call it a day.
   I decided to *stop / try again tomorrow*.
4 I was having a hard time.
   It was difficult for me. / It took a long time.
5 I decided to let myself go.
   I decided to *stop swimming / try again*.
6 I scrambled onto the beach.
   I moved *quickly / slowly*.

4 Discuss the questions with your partner.

1 Sala talks about three decisions he made. What were they and what were the consequences of each one?
2 Sala describes how he feels about the sea. Do you think what he says is unusual? Why?
3 Read the last sentence. What do you think Sala means?
4 Do you think the title of the article is a good one? Why?

Critical thinking reading between the lines

5 Do you think these statements are true (T) or false (F)? Why?

1 The Costa Brava is dangerous for swimmers.
2 Enric Sala likes to take risks.
3 He was lucky to escape with his life.
4 He has recovered from the experience now.
5 He respects the sea more than he did before.

Word focus *get*

6 Look at the verbs in bold in these sentences. Find expressions with *get* in the article that match the verbs. Then rewrite the sentences with *get*.

1 I **entered** the pool.
2 The weather **didn't improve**.
3 I couldn't **reach** the shore.
4 I wasn't **moving towards** the land.
5 We **receive** so much from nature.
6 I'd **escaped from** that dangerous situation.

7 Write six other sentences about your own experiences using the expressions with *get* from the article.

Speaking

8 Think of a story about an unforgettable experience you have read about or had. Use the points to plan your story.

- the place / situation
- the people involved
- the weather / any other relevant conditions
- what happened
- why it happened
- how it happened
- what happened next

9 Use your notes to practice telling the story. Then work in small groups and tell your story.

> *This happened a few years ago. I was coming home from work when I saw an old friend.*

Love & death in the sea
and in the sea

The sea has almost killed me a couple of times. It wasn't her fault; it was mine, for not respecting her. I still remember the last time, a stormy day off the Costa Brava of Spain, in early summer 2008. Every time I think about it, my heart races and my guts jump to my throat.

The cove where I used to swim every day was hit by a storm with strong eastern winds. The turquoise, transparent waters quickly transformed into a dirty soup of sand and cold gray water. Unfriendly waves were breaking in chaotic patterns. But beyond the surf zone, the sea seemed swimmable. In a moment of Catalan bravado, I put on my swimsuit, mask, and fins, and got into the water. It was crazy, but I did it. I swallowed mouthfuls of sand and salt while I was trying to break through the surf zone. Unpleasantly fighting, I swam—I still don't know why—for twenty minutes. The storm got worse and I decided to call it a day. I turned to swim back. Then I realized I couldn't get to the beach.

Waves were breaking all around me. I tried to bodysurf one wave to the shore, but it collapsed suddenly and took me down under the water. When I surfaced to take a breath, I turned around and a second wave hit me just as hard, taking me down again. I hit the sandy bottom. I pushed myself up, but once again, waves were coming and I couldn't rest or breathe. I was caught in the surf zone, with waves pushing me out and a current pulling me in. I wasn't getting any closer to the beach.

The sea is our mother, sister, and home, and as such I love her. We get so much from the sea: life, oxygen, food. She regulates the climate and she makes ours a wonderful life. We should thank the sea, the ocean, every day. Without the ocean and all the life in her, our planet would be much poorer. But on this day, I was having a hard time feeling grateful.

After a few more attempts, I decided to let go and give up the fight. I took a deep breath. The next wave took me down and forward. I hit the bottom with my back. I rolled over, hit my head, and after what seemed the longest minute of my life, I found myself lying in a foot of water. I scrambled onto the beach. I'd gotten out, but my whole body was sore, as if a gang of boxers had punched me viciously. I sat on the beach, breathless, watching the sea and feeling lucky to be alive. I walked home slowly, ears down like a beaten dog.

Some days the sea wants us and some days she doesn't. Since that day, I have not been to the sea when she does not want me. I have learned my lesson. I now thank the sea every day the surface is calm, the waters are clear, and diving is easy. And I ask for forgiveness every time I dive and see no fish.

> **bravado** (n) /brəˈvɑdoʊ/ false bravery
> **cove** (n) /koʊv/ a small bay on the coast
> **gang** (n) /gæŋ/ a group of people (usually has a negative meaning)
> **grateful** (adj) /ˈgreɪtfəl/ thankful and appreciative
> **guts** (n) /gʌts/ stomach and intestines

3d No way!

Real life telling stories

1 Work in groups. Which of these statements (a–e) are true for you? Tell your group.

   a When I'm in a group, I listen more than I talk.
   b I'm always telling funny stories about things that happen to me.
   c I like jokes, but I can never remember the punch line.
   d I'm hopeless at telling stories, but I'm a good listener.
   e People say I exaggerate, but they always laugh at my stories.

2 Look at the photo. Which group of words (A or B) do you think are from the story of the photo? Working in pairs, compare your ideas and explain your reasons.

A looking after it	**B** our house was like a zoo
food and water	jump in the air
empty cage	above the kitchen sink
searched	a lid on a tank
everywhere	there was some water
taking a bath	in it

3 🎵 **11** Listen to two stories. Which one matches the photo? What would a photo of the other story show?

4 🎵 **11** Look at the expressions for telling stories. Then listen to the story again and mark the expressions the speakers use.

> ▶ **TELLING STORIES**
>
> **Beginning a story**
> Did I ever tell you about… ?
> I remember once,…
> A couple of years ago,…
> You'll never believe what happened once…
>
> **Saying when things happened**
> after we saw…
> after a few days
> a couple of weeks later
> one day
> all of a sudden
> suddenly
> immediately
> then
> the next thing was
> while I was…
> during the night

5 Only one of the stories is true. Which one do you think it is?

6 Pronunciation *was* and *were*

a 🎵 **12** Listen to the sentences from the stories in Exercise 3. Notice the sound /ə/ in *was* and *were*.

b 🎵 **12** Listen again and then repeat these sentences. Pay attention to how you say *was* and *were*.

   1 Especially when someone was doing the dishes.
   2 They were lying in the sink!
   3 We were looking after this friend's parrot.
   4 I was going around the house calling "Polly!"

7 Working in pairs, choose one of the stories from Exercise 3 and each take a role. Use the audioscript on page 174 and practice the conversation. Change roles and repeat with the other story.

8 Work in pairs.

Student A: Tell your partner about something that happened to you or to someone you know. At least one part of the story should be untrue. Use the expressions for telling stories to help you.

Student B: Try to guess which part of your partner's story is untrue.

> *Did I ever tell you about the time my uncle went fishing?*

> *No, you didn't.*

3e What a weekend!

Writing a blog post

1 Do you keep a blog or know someone who does? What kind of things do people write about in personal blogs? And in professional blogs?

2 Read the blog post and answer the questions.

1 What is the topic of this blog post?
2 What do you think *beach stuff* refers to?
3 Who do you think Ellie, Louis, and Oscar are?

3 Put the main events of the story (a–g) in the correct order.

a Ellie, Louis, and Oscar **ran** to the water.
b The sun **started to shine**.
c There was a storm.
d A ship lost a cargo of sneakers.
e They **got** into the car.
f They **picked up** things to take to the beach.
g They **went** to the beach.

4 Writing skill interesting language

a Compare the post with the sentences in Exercise 3. Which verbs does James use instead of the verbs in bold in Exercise 3? Why?

b Circle the verbs and adjectives James uses instead of these words.

| raining | full of people | looking |
| arrived | holding | |

c Read the sentences. Which words do you think are missing? Then complete the sentences with the words in the box.

1 The kids _____ along the street.
2 I felt _____ after my walk.
3 The weather was _____ hot.
4 We _____ up the river bank with difficulty.
5 I _____ along the beach in no hurry.
6 At the end of the game, we _____ on the sand.

| boiling | collapsed | exhausted |
| raced | scrambled | wandered |

5 Think about a recent weekend or one when something unusual happened. Make notes of the main events in your weekend. Then add notes with background information.

The calm after the storm

It was pouring rain all weekend, so we spent almost the whole time indoors trying to entertain the kids. Then, unexpectedly, the sun came out late on Sunday afternoon. We grabbed our beach stuff, jumped into the car, and headed down to the bay. When we got there, we realized that everyone had had the same idea! The beach was packed. But everyone was staring out to sea and picking stuff up off the sand. Ellie, Louis, and Oscar rushed down to the water's edge, full of excitement. It turned out that a ship had lost its cargo in Saturday's storm. Five containers of Nike sneakers had washed up on the beach! Everyone was clutching odd shoes, looking for the other one to make a pair! What a strange weekend!

Written by James   Feb 28, 11:14PM

See older posts

6 Write a first draft of a blog post about your weekend. Then look at the vocabulary you have used. Make any changes to make your post as interesting as you can. Use these questions to check it.

- Have you used different past tenses correctly?
- Have you used interesting vocabulary?

7 Work in pairs. Exchange posts. Has your partner written an interesting post?

One village makes a difference

The Yamuna River is the city's main source of drinking water.

Before you watch

1 Work in groups. Look at the photo of the Yamuna River in northern India and discuss the questions.

1 Why do you think the river looks like this?
2 What problems do you think this creates for the people of New Delhi?
3 Where do you think people who live far from this river get their water from?

2 The video shows people in northern India using water for a variety of things. Write down five things you think you will see.

While you watch

3 Watch the video and check your ideas from Exercise 2.

4 Watch the first part of the video (to 02:21). Are these sentences true (T) or false (F)?

1 Fifty million gallons of waste are thrown into the Yamuna River every day.
2 Fourteen million people in and around Delhi get their water from water tankers.
3 There is never enough water for everyone.
4 The people of New Delhi need about one million gallons of water a day.
5 The residents of the city are surviving on a quarter of the water they need.
6 Rich people have their own supply of water.
7 The monsoon season replaces all the water used during the year.
8 Everyone agrees that new dams are the only solution to the water shortage.

5 Watch the second part of the video (02:23 to the end). Put the stages of making traditional dams and the results in the correct order.

a the level of water under the ground rises
b put down a layer of porous stone, earth, and clay
c create wells to irrigate farms
d make small pits or holes near the dams
e make small earthen dams of stone and rock

6 Complete these sentences with words from the glossary. Then watch the video again and check your answers.

1 The heavy _____ that fills the sky is so unclean that it's difficult to see the city.
2 When villagers reach a _____ , they often have to drink next to their animals.
3 India's dams have contributed to the water shortage by drying up _____ and wells.
4 We're building water _____ and dams to save rainwater.
5 The _____ methods of Alwar aren't practical for New Delhi.

After you watch

7 **Roleplay** **talking about a development project.**

Work in pairs.

Student A: You are Rajendra Singh. Read the instructions below and make notes.

- You are going to meet with an official from the United Nations to discuss a project.
- Welcome your visitor, explain your project, and answer the visitor's questions.

Student B: You are a United Nations official. Read the instructions below.

- You are going to visit a traditional dam project in India.
- Make a list of questions to ask Rajendra Singh, the project organizer.
- When you are ready, say hello, ask Mr. Singh to explain the project, and ask him your questions.

8 Work in pairs. Discuss these questions.

1 Where do cities in your country get their water?
2 Have there ever been any water shortages where you live? What effect did they have?
3 What can we do to protect Earth's water for future generations?

---

available (adj) /əˈveɪləbəl/ ready for use
clay (n) /kleɪ/ thick, sticky earth
dam (n) /dæm/ a wall built across a river or stream
earthen (adj) /ˈɜrθən/ made of earth
industrial waste (n) /ɪnˈdʌstriəl ˈweɪst/ chemical substances that factories throw away
irrigate (v) /ˈɪrɪˌɡeɪt/ water plants or fields
lifeless (adj) /ˈlaɪflɪs/ dead
monsoon (n) /mɑnˈsun/ a season of heavy tropical rain
porous (adj) /ˈpɔrəs/ allowing water to pass through
prosperous (adj) /ˈprɑspərəs/ wealthy
replace (v) /rɪˈpleɪs/ put back

reservoir (n) /ˈrezərˌvwɑr/ an artificial lake
rise (v) /raɪz/ go higher
river bed (n) /ˈrɪvərˌbed/ the bottom of a river
shortage (n) /ˈʃɔrtɪdʒ/ when there is not enough of something
shower (n) /ˈʃaʊər/ a short period of rain
small-scale (adj) /ˈsmɔl ˈskeɪl/ not very big
smog (n) /smɑg/ a kind of fog caused by pollution
source (n) /ˈsɔrs/ the place something comes from
store (v) /ˈstɔr/ save for later use
well (n) /wel/ a deep round hole in the ground that people make to get water

UNIT 3 REVIEW

Grammar

1 Work in pairs. Look at the photo. Have you ever done anything like this? Would you like to?

I ^{1} *learned* to surf a few years ago when I ^{2} *was* in my teens. My dad ^{3} *paid* for lessons, as a present, because I ^{4} *just passed* some important exams. It ^{5} *was* a sunny weekend in June and the whole first day ^{6} *went by* and I ^{7} *didn't manage* one successful ride. All my friends ^{8} *watched* and of course I ^{9} *wanted* to impress them. I eventually ^{10} *paddled out* for my last attempt of the day when the sun ^{11} *set* over the bay. I ^{12} *scrambled* onto the board and for the first time I ^{13} *didn't fall off* right away. I ^{14} *just got up* on the board when someone almost ^{15} *crashed* right into me! But I ^{16} *stayed* on!

2 With your partner, change the verbs in the story to the past continuous or past perfect where appropriate. Do you think the photo illustrates this story? Why?

I CAN	
talk about a sequence of events in the past (simple past, past perfect)	☐
describe the background to past events (past continuous)	☐

Vocabulary

3 Rewrite the words with the missing vowels to give names for places with water. Race your partner to see who can finish first. How many examples of each place can you name?

Example:
lake – Lake Nasser

lk	pl	s
mrn	rsrvr	strm
cn	rvr	wtrfll

4 Work on your own. Choose the two activities you think best match each category (1–4). Then work in pairs to discuss your reasons.

1 people find this relaxing
2 people do this to get a thrill
3 it's best to do this with other people
4 people do this on weekends

diving	fishing	jet-skiing	kayaking
rafting	rowing	sailing	snorkeling
surfing	swimming	water-skiing	windsurfing

5 Work in pairs. Discuss the questions.

1 How many times did you use water yesterday? What did you use it for?
2 Do you think you waste water? Why?
3 Why is it important not to waste water?

I CAN	
talk about water sports	☐
talk about water use	☐

Real life

6 Work in groups. Tell a story starting with this sentence. Take turns adding a sentence to the story, using one of these expressions.

Did I ever tell you about the time my cat ate my homework?

a couple of… later	one day
after a few…	suddenly
all of a sudden	the next thing was
during the…	then
immediately	while I was…

7 Use one of these sentences to tell another story.

I remember once, I was waiting at the bus stop.

A couple of years ago, I went for a job interview.

You'll never believe what happened once when I was taking an exam.

I CAN	
tell a story	☐
say when things happened in a sequence of events	☐

Speaking

8 Work in groups. A person was about to start a challenging new job when a friend commented "You'll either sink or swim." What do you think the expression means? Talk about times in the past when you have faced a challenge. How did you feel? What happened in the end?

Unit 4 Opportunities

Schoolchildren

FEATURES

1 Work in pairs. Look at the photo. How old do you think the children are? What do you think they study in school? Do you think they like school?

2 Did you want to do any of these jobs when you were a child?

athlete	ballerina	firefighter	pilot
movie star	police officer	rock star	scientist
train conductor	vet		

3 Which words describe the jobs in Exercise 2?

badly paid	boring	dangerous	demanding
dirty	exciting	glamorous	responsible
rewarding	routine	satisfying	secure
stressful	well-paid		

4 Work in pairs. Answer the questions about yourself.

   a What job have you always wanted to do?
   b Which job do you do now or plan to do?
   c How would you describe your dream job?

4a Fast lane to the future

Reading

1 Work in pairs. Look at the title of the article, the photo, and the map. What do you think the article is about?

2 Read the article and check your ideas from Exercise 1.

3 Complete the table.

Name	Job	Employer
Meena Shekaran	1	an importer
Tamil Selvan	2	3 ....
Kashinath Manna	4	self-employed
Morten Andersen	5	6 ....

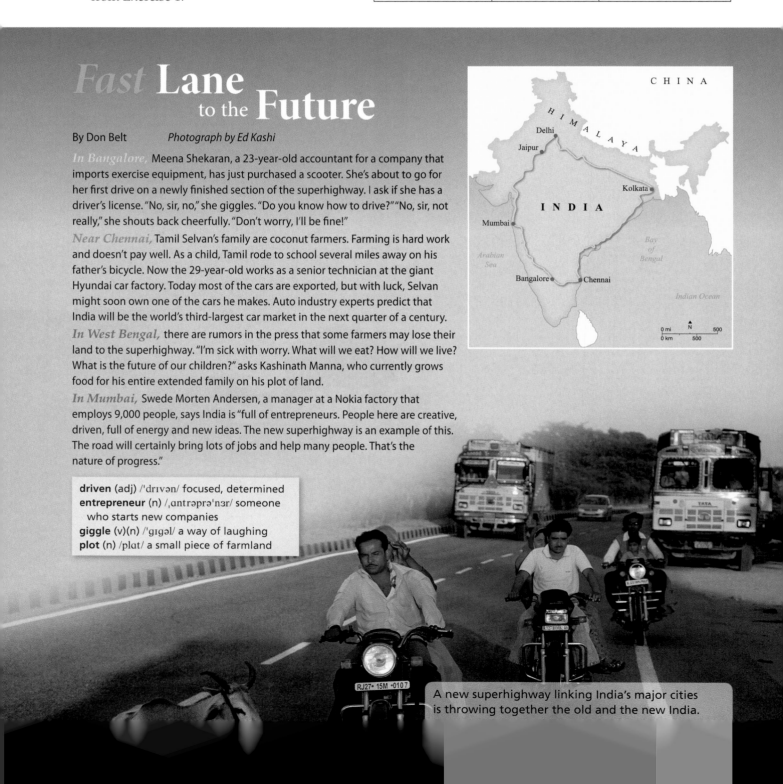

Fast **Lane** to the **Future**

By Don Belt   *Photograph by Ed Kashi*

In Bangalore, Meena Shekaran, a 23-year-old accountant for a company that imports exercise equipment, has just purchased a scooter. She's about to go for her first drive on a newly finished section of the superhighway. I ask if she has a driver's license. "No, sir, no," she giggles. "Do you know how to drive?" "No, sir, not really," she shouts back cheerfully. "Don't worry, I'll be fine!"

Near Chennai, Tamil Selvan's family are coconut farmers. Farming is hard work and doesn't pay well. As a child, Tamil rode to school several miles away on his father's bicycle. Now the 29-year-old works as a senior technician at the giant Hyundai car factory. Today most of the cars are exported, but with luck, Selvan might soon own one of the cars he makes. Auto industry experts predict that India will be the world's third-largest car market in the next quarter of a century.

In West Bengal, there are rumors in the press that some farmers may lose their land to the superhighway. "I'm sick with worry. What will we eat? How will we live? What is the future of our children?" asks Kashinath Manna, who currently grows food for his entire extended family on his plot of land.

In Mumbai, Swede Morten Andersen, a manager at a Nokia factory that employs 9,000 people, says India is "full of entrepreneurs. People here are creative, driven, full of energy and new ideas. The new superhighway is an example of this. The road will certainly bring lots of jobs and help many people. That's the nature of progress."

driven (adj) /ˈdrɪvən/ focused, determined
entrepreneur (n) /ˌɑntrəprəˈnɜr/ someone who starts new companies
giggle (v)(n) /ˈgɪgəl/ a way of laughing
plot (n) /plɑt/ a small piece of farmland

A new superhighway linking India's major cities is throwing together the old and the new India.

4 Read the article again and complete the sentences.

1 .... believes that the road represents progress in India.
2 .... has bought a new vehicle to drive on the road.
3 .... is worried about the future.
4 .... makes cars that might end up on the road.

5 Do you think the new road is a good thing or a bad thing? Why?

Grammar predictions

▶ PREDICTIONS WITH *WILL*

The future	will (not) may (not) might (not) could will certainly / definitely / probably certainly / definitely / probably won't	be difficult.

For more information and practice, see page 160.

6 Look at the grammar box. Which verb forms from the box are in the article? Underline them in the article.

7 Look at the sentences with the underlined verb forms in the article. Answer the questions for each sentence.

1 Who makes the prediction?
2 Is the person 100 percent sure of his/her prediction?

8 Cross out the option that is not logical, as in the example.

1 Meena has bought a scooter. She *might / will / ~~won't~~* learn to drive soon.
2 The road links the major cities. It *could / may not / will* affect many people.
3 Ravi isn't very good at his job. He *might / might not / will* get a promotion.
4 Hyundai is building a new factory. They *could / might not / will* need more workers.
5 We haven't seen the plans for the road. It *may / might not / will* go near our house.
6 I get bored at work. I *may / may not / might* look for a new job.

9 Look at the sentences in Exercise 8 again. What is the difference between the correct options in each case?

10 Write predictions, as in the example, using one of the options. Then work as a class and compare your sentences.

1 Meena / not crash (probably / certainly)
   Meena probably won't crash on her first drive.
2 Tamil Selvan / buy a car (definitely / probably)
3 Kashinath Manna's life / not change (definitely / might)
4 the Nokia factory / expand (certainly / probably)
5 job opportunities / increase (definitely / might)
6 traveling around / be easier (certainly / probably)
7 people's standard of living / improve (certainly / might)

Vocabulary *job* and *work*

11 Look at the examples from the article (a–c). Then complete the sentences (1–8) with the correct form of *job* or *work*.

a Farming is hard work and doesn't pay well.
b …the 29-year-old works as a senior technician…
c …the road will bring lots of jobs…

1 Where do you .... ?
2 Do you have an interesting .... ?
3 Do you usually have a lot of .... ?
4 Is your company good to .... for?
5 Want to go out later? I get off .... at 5.
6 Don't use that phone. It doesn't ....
7 I'll be home late tonight. There are a few .... to finish here.
8 "Is your dad around?" "No, he's at ...."

12 Work in pairs. Take turns asking and answering questions 1–4 from Exercise 11.

Speaking

13 Work in pairs. Discuss and agree on six predictions about your own country or town. Talk about these issues or use your own ideas.

- economy
- environment
- jobs
- local politics
- prices
- roads

I think the new shopping center will definitely make my life easier.

You're probably right, but how will it affect the small stores around here?

4b What's next?

Devi
Wayne

Elisabeth

Sahera with her friends

Listening

1 Work in pairs. Have you made any important decisions recently? Tell your partner about one of them.

> *I've decided to change careers.*
> *I don't want to work in an office.*

2 🎵 **13** Listen to part of a radio program about International Women's Day. Choose the correct option for the three women featured in the program.

1 Devi *works / studies*.
2 Devi wants to be *a boss / a nurse*.
3 Elisabeth *has a job / doesn't have a job*.
4 Elisabeth intends to *leave work / retire*.
5 Sahera has just *started college / graduated from college*.
6 Sahera plans to *stay in Kabul / leave Kabul*.

3 🎵 **13** Listen again and correct the factual mistakes.

1 Devi isn't going to stay at home forever.
2 Devi is taking a test tomorrow.
3 Elisabeth is going to start a new job.
4 Elisabeth is meeting her new boss on Wednesday.
5 Sahera's friend is going to work in the United States.
6 Sahera's friend is leaving Kabul next month.

4 Which of the women has decided what she is going to do? Who doesn't know yet?

Grammar **future forms**

5 Look at the audioscript on page 175. Find the following.

1 something Devi has already decided to do
2 something Devi has arranged to do
3 something Devi decides to do as she is speaking

6 Read what Elisabeth and Sahera say in the audioscript. Underline more sentences like those in Exercise 5.

1 Present continuous
I'm taking the exam next month.
2 *will*
Just a moment, I'll get you some.
3 *going to*
I'm going to start my own business.

For more information and practice, see page 161.

7 Look at the grammar box. Match the verb forms
(1–3) with their uses (a–c).

a   a plan or intention decided before the moment
of speaking
b   a decision made at the moment of speaking
c   an arrangement to do something at a specified
(or understood) time in the future

8 Choose the correct option.

I left school last month.
¹ *I'll take / I'm taking*
the summer off, but
on September 3 **²** *I'll
start / I'm starting* as an
apprentice in a garage.
³ *I'll take / I'm going to
take* an evening course
too. That starts in
October. I'm not sure
how **⁴** *I'm managing /
I'm going to manage*!
I'm lucky—some of my friends don't know
what **⁵** *they are doing / they are going to do*. My
mom thinks **⁶** *I'm being / I'm going to be* a great
mechanic. Maybe **⁷** *I'll have / I'm going to have*
my own garage one day.

9 Complete the responses with the most logical
future form. Then work in pairs. Compare and
discuss your answers.

1   A: Do you have any plans for when you
leave college?
B: Yes, I _____ (take) a year off.

2   A: I can't decide what to do.
B: It's OK, I _____ (help) you.

3   A: Is it true that Samira is leaving?
B: Yeah, she _____ (get) married next
month.

4   A: Did you enroll in evening classes?
B: Yes, _____ (go) to my first class
tonight.

5   A: I can't get this can open!
B: Here, give it to me. I _____
(open) it.

Vocabulary education

10 How do these events affect one another? Complete
the timelines with these expressions. More than
one answer is possible.

take a (training) course   get bad grades
fail an exam/a test   pass/retake an exam/
                                a test
get a degree in…   stay in school

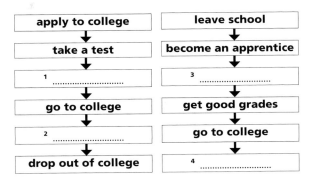

apply to college	leave school
↓	↓
take a test	become an apprentice
↓	↓
1	3 ....
↓	↓
go to college	get good grades
↓	↓
2	go to college
↓	↓
drop out of college	4 ....

11 Work in pairs. Discuss these questions.

1   How similar or different are the events in
Exercise 10 to your own experience?
2   What kinds of factors influence these decisions?
3   What plans do people you know have?

▶ **WORDBUILDING phrasal verbs**

We often use phrasal verbs when talking about our actions.
drop out   stay in

12 What will your own educational path be like in the
next two years? Write your own timeline. Then get
together with a partner and explain your plans.

Speaking

13 Work in pairs. You need to meet several times for
a project for your English class. Find dates when
you can get together.

*What are you up to next week? Maybe
we can get together early in the week.*

OK. Do you have any plans for Monday?

4c A better life?

Reading

1 Work in groups. What kind of things happen in an economic boom and in an economic crisis? Give examples.

> *In an economic boom, there is more work.*

> *Yes, and people can buy more luxury goods.*

2 Read the article on page 51 quickly. Which paragraphs talk about these topics?

   a training and education
   b China and the world
   c the movement of people
   d new towns

3 Read the first paragraph of the article. Put these things (a–f) in the order they appear in a new town in China.

   a basic stalls
   b cellphone companies
   c clothing stores
   d construction work   *1*
   e entrepreneurs
   f female factory workers

4 Read the rest of the article. Are the sentences true (T) or false (F)?

   1 Most of the population is young.
   2 About ten million people a year migrate to the cities.
   3 Few school drop-outs in China are interested in higher education.
   4 It's difficult to find training courses in factory towns.
   5 So far China has focused on making products for foreign markets.

5 Work in pairs. What do these sentences from the last paragraph mean?

> Nobody in the developed world should criticize China without taking a look in the mirror.

> There's nothing foreign about the materialistic dreams of the average Chinese worker.

Critical thinking arguments

6 The title of the article is *A better life?* Read these sentences from the text. Decide if what they describe is positive (P), negative (N), or both (B).

   1 Most people in China have seen their standard of living go up in recent years.
   2 Social scientists predict that the urban population will be 60 percent by 2030.
   3 Clearly there are environmental costs from China's rapid growth.

7 Which of these statements (a–c) describes the author's opinion of China?

   a The changes described will probably be better.
   b The changes described will probably be bad.
   c The changes could be good or bad.

8 Work as a class. What things do you think make "a better life"?

Vocabulary and speaking pay and benefits

9 Work in pairs. Read each sentence and think of a profession it describes.

> *Doctors work long hours!*

   1 They work **long hours**.
   2 They get a lot of **paid vacation**.
   3 They get regular **pay raises**.
   4 Their **salary** is excellent.
   5 They can choose to work **flex time hours** if they need to.
   6 There are lots of opportunities for **promotion**.
   7 They often have to work **overtime**.
   8 They get a generous **retirement package.**

10 Put the words in bold in Exercise 9 into three groups: *money* (M), *hours* (H), and *benefits* (B). Then add these words to the groups.

bonuses	free language classes
clocking in and out	health insurance
company car	part-time hours
discounts on company products	hourly wage

11 Tell your partner about your ideal job. Talk about pay, conditions, and responsibilities. What's the most important aspect of the job for you?

> *Well, my ideal job is working outdoors.*

A better life?

China's expectations are rising, with no end in sight. What's next?
By Peter Hessler
Photographs by Fritz Hoffmann

In Shenzhen, factory workers pose for a portrait at the morning shift change.

The beginning of a Chinese factory town is always the same: in the beginning, nearly everybody is a construction worker. The growing economy means that everything moves fast and new industrial districts rise in several stages. Those early laborers are men who have migrated from a rural village. Immediately they are joined by small entrepreneurs. These pioneers sell meat, fruit, and vegetables from stalls, and later, when the first real stores appear, they stock construction materials. After that, cellphone companies arrive, selling prepaid phonecards to migrants. (One popular product is called the Homesick Card.) When the factories start production,

you start to see women. Young women have a reputation for being hard-working. After the arrival of the women, the clothing stores appear. An American poet once described an industrial town in the US as "springing up, like the enchanted palaces of the Arabian tales, as it were in a single night." Today it's the factory towns of China that seem to belong to another world. The human energy is amazing: the courageous entrepreneurs, the quick-moving builders, the young migrants. A combination of past problems and present-day opportunities has created an extremely motivated population. Most people in China have seen their standard of living go up in recent years.

The size of the population is both a strength and a challenge to China. Of its 1.3 billion people, 72 percent are between the ages of 16 and 64. The movement of people from the country-side to the cities has transformed

China into the world's factory floor. In 1978, there were only 172 million urban residents. Now there are 577 million. Social scientists predict that the urban population will be 60 percent of the total population by 2030. Each year about ten million rural Chinese move to the cities, so the factories have a constant labor supply.

Chinese schools have been very successful. The literacy rate is over 90 percent. The next step is to develop higher education. Many people are looking for better training. In a Chinese factory town, there are many private classes: English, typing, technical. In Zhejiang, I met Luo Shouyun, who had spent a quarter of his wages on training. Now he is a master machinist, with a salary that makes him "middle class." Another young man had learned Arabic in order to translate for Middle Eastern buyers.

Clearly there are environmental costs from China's rapid growth. Collaboration between China and other countries will be crucial in managing environmental problems. Nobody in the developed world should criticize China without taking a look in the mirror. The nation has become successful by making products for overseas consumers. There's nothing foreign about the materialistic dreams of the average Chinese worker.

Individual portraits in Beijing on Chinese National Day

literacy rate (n) /ˈlɪtərəsi ˌreɪt/ the number of people who can read and write
materialistic (adj) /məˌtɪəriəˈlɪstɪk/ interested in possessions and consumer goods
migrant (n) /ˈmaɪɡrənt/ someone who moves around, often for work
overseas (adj) /ˈoʊvərˈsiz/ foreign, from another country

4d Would you mind...?

Vocabulary job requirements

> **Research Assistant**
>
> **NaturalHistoryNet**
>
> **Full-time position + benefits. Starting 12-month contract.**
>
> *You will be responsible for*
> - assisting the Research Coordinator on a variety of movie projects.
> - managing movie production materials such as scripts and footage.
> - dealing with questions related to current and past projects.
>
> *You will have*
> - a degree in a relevant subject.
> - preferably 1–2 years' experience in movie production.
> - excellent database and research skills.
>
> *You will be*
> - organized and independent.
> - able to meet strict deadlines.
> - good at working under pressure.
>
> **Send resume and cover letter to: jobs@NHNTV.com**
> **Application deadline: June 15**

1 Read the job ad and find the following.

1 responsibilities
2 deadline for applications
3 skills and qualifications required
4 personal qualities required

2 Which of these qualities would be useful for the job in the ad?

conscientious	creative	energetic
hard-working	methodical	self-confident

3 Work in pairs. Choose three jobs you know something about. What are the most important requirements for those jobs? Compare your ideas.

Real life making and responding to requests

4 🔘 **14** Listen to two friends talk about the ad. Answer the questions.

1 Does he meet all the requirements?
2 Is his resume ready?
3 What will he need for the interview?

5 🔘 **14** Look at the expressions for making and responding to requests. Listen to the conversation again and mark the expressions you hear.

> **▶ MAKING AND RESPONDING TO REQUESTS**
>
> **Making requests**
> Is it all right if I give you as my reference?
> Would it be OK to borrow your suit?
> Is it OK to take your car?
> Would it be all right if I used your phone?
>
> Would you mind checking my application form?
> Do you mind helping me with my resume?
>
> Could you give me a ride to the interview?
> Can you have a look at my cover letter?
> Will you be able to do it today?
>
> **Responding to requests**
> | | |
> |---|---|
> | Of course (not). | Yes, I will. |
> | I'm not sure about that. | Sure, no problem. |

6 Would you like to do a job like the one in the ad? Why?

7 Pronunciation weak and strong auxiliary verbs

a 🔘 **15** Listen to this exchange and repeat it. Notice how the auxiliary verb *will* is not stressed in the full question and is stressed in the response.

A: Will you be able to do it today?
B: Yes, I will.

b Match the questions (1–6) with the responses (a–f). Check your answers with your instructor, then practice the exchanges in pairs.

1 Are you going to apply for the job?
2 Will he help you with your resume?
3 Are they still advertising that job?
4 Does she meet our requirements?
5 Will it be an all-day interview?
6 Is it OK to call your cell?

a I don't think she does.
b I think it might.
c No, they aren't.
d Of course he will.
e Yes, I think I will.
f Yes, of course it is.

8 Work in pairs. You are going to act out 90-second conversations in different situations. Turn to page 155.

4e I am enclosing my resume

Writing a cover letter

1 Work in pairs. Have you ever applied for a job in these ways? Tell your partner.

> a resume   a phone call
> a letter   an application form
> a personal contact

2 Read the cover letter. Mark the information it includes. What (if anything) can you omit if you send an email?

> a reference to your resume
> the date
> the name and address of the person you
>   are writing to
> the reason for your letter
> your address
> your interest in the position
> your phone number
> your education, experience, and skills

3 Compare the letter to the style you use in your country. Answer the questions.

1 Is the layout different? How?
2 Does it include the same information?
3 Is the information in the main part of the letter sequenced in the same way?

4 Writing skill formal style

a A formal letter in English uses these conventions. Underline examples of each one in the letter.

- concise sentences
- formal phrases to begin sentences
- no contractions
- standard opening and closing phrases

b Rewrite the sentences in a more formal style.

1 I'm finishing my degree soon.
2 Give me a call.
3 I was looking through the paper and I saw your ad, and I thought it looked really interesting.
4 My phone number is on my resume, which I've also sent you.
5 I'll be free in August.

---

14 Washington Street
Brighton, MA 02135
June 7, 2014

NHN TV
1200 Commonwealth Ave.
Boston, MA 02101

Dear Sir or Madam,

I am writing in reply to your advertisement in the Daily Herald for the post of Research Assistant. I will graduate in Digital Media this month from Boston University. I have experience in video production and post-production, having worked part-time in the university television station for the last year.

I consider myself to be hard-working and organized in my work. As part of my job, I was responsible for planning schedules and archiving past programs.

I am available for an interview at any time and can start work after July. I am willing to relocate if necessary.

I am enclosing my resume that gives full details of my education, work experience, and skills as well as my contact details.

I look forward to hearing from you.

Yours sincerely,

Mani Banerjee

---

5 Write a cover letter to go with a job application. Follow the layout and style of the letter above.

6 Exchange letters with your partner. Use these questions to check your partner's letter.

- Is it clear how to contact this person?
- Is the style appropriate?
- Does the person sound like a good candidate?

7 On the basis of the letter your partner has written, would you give him/her an interview? Explain your reasons.

Confucianism in China

China is one of the largest and oldest countries in the world.

Before you watch

1 Work in groups. Look at the photos. Write down everything you know about China and about Confucius. You have three minutes. Then compare what you have written with other groups.

2 You are going to watch a video about China. Write down one image that you think:

1 you will definitely see.
2 you might see.
3 you definitely won't see.

While you watch

3 Check your answers from Exercises 1 and 2.

4 Watch the first part of the video (to 01:59). Choose the correct option to complete the sentences about the early history of China.

1 Confucius lived from:
   a 551 to 479 BCE.   b 500 to 600 BCE.

2 Around 500 BCE, central China was governed by the .... dynasty.
   a Han   b Zhou

3 The rulers were:
   a weak.   b very unhappy.

4 Local warlords:
   a fought for land and power.
   b fought for justice in the country.

5 Confucius traveled across China to convince people:
   a to fight against the warlords.
   b that his ideas could restore order.

6 Three hundred years after Confucius died, the Han dynasty:
   a adopted his philosophy.
   b banned his teachings.

5 Watch the second part of the video (02:02 to the end). Number the sayings in the order you hear them.

   a Virtue is the root; wealth is the result.
   b Is it not pleasant to learn with a constant perseverance and application?
   c A youth should be respectful of his elders.

6 Watch the video again and complete the sentences with words from the glossary.

1 Millions of Chinese people .... a rich history that has lasted for thousands of years.
2 The country of China was .... up in a dark period of war and unhappiness.
3 Traditionally, sons .... the family name and support their parents.
4 Throughout the history of China, an education has been an opportunity to .... in the world.
5 Because Confucianism is often associated with China's past, many people aren't .... of its influence on present-day society.

After you watch

7 Roleplay **talking about a country's culture**

Work in pairs.

Student A: You are Chinese. Make notes about the three aspects of culture below, then explain to your partner how Chinese culture is different from his/hers.

Student B: Your partner is Chinese and studying abroad. Write questions to ask about how the three aspects below are different from the culture in your country.

   • respect   • learning   • virtue and wealth

Act out the conversation, then change roles.

8 Work in groups and discuss these questions.

1 Do you agree with what Confucius says about youth, education, and wealth? Why?
2 Do you think Confucius's philosophy has anything to offer your country? What in particular?

---

attain (v) /ə'teɪn/ get
be aware of (v) /'bi ə'weər əv/ know about
be caught up in (v) /'bi kɔt 'ʌp ɪn/ be in the middle of
carry on (v) /'kæri 'ɑn/ continue
conduct (n) /'kɑndʌkt/ a way of behaving
convince (v) /kən'vɪns/ make someone believe something
dutiful (adj) /'dutɪfəl/ doing what you are supposed to do
dynasty (n) /'daɪnəsti/ a family that rules a country for several generations
ethical (adj) /'eθɪkəl/ relating to what is right and wrong
foundation (n) /faʊn'deɪʃən/ base
govern (v) /'gʌvərn/ administer a country
harmony (n) /'hɑrməni/ a state when people live together without problems
in decline (adv) /'ɪn dɪ'klaɪn/ becoming weaker, poorer

joy (n) /dʒɔɪ/ happiness
move up (v) /'muv 'ʌp/ progress
perseverance (n) /ˌpərsə'vɪərəns/ the capacity to keep going in difficult conditions
prosper (v) /'prɑspər/ be successful
respectful (adj) /rɪ'spektfəl/ polite and obedient
restore (v) /rɪ'stɔr/ bring back
root (n) /rut/ base
ruler (n) /'rulər/ the head of a country
share (v) /ʃeər/ have something in common
subject (n) /'sʌbdʒəkt/ a person who lives in a country that has a ruler
virtue (n) /'vɜrtʃu/ behaving in a moral way
warlord (n) /'wɔrˌlɔrd/ the leader of a private army
wealth (n) /welθ/ a large amount of money

UNIT 4 REVIEW

Grammar

1 Work in pairs. Look at the photo of student chefs in China cooking vegetables. What do you think they are thinking about?

2 Complete the comments with one word. Which do you think were made by the Chinese student chefs in the photo?

1 "I'm sure nobody _____ be able to eat this!"
2 "I think I _____ change jobs soon."
3 "I _____ having a drink on my next break."
4 "This _____ definitely impress the diners."
5 "I _____ be the best chef in the country."
6 "My parents are going _____ be proud of me."
7 "This may _____ turn out as I expected."
8 "Wow, my hat is _____ to catch fire."
9 "My friends _____ believe me when I tell them about my day."
10 "I'm _____ take-out for dinner tonight."

3 Work in pairs. Imagine you are the students in the photo. Ask each other about your plans for when the course ends.

I CAN	
make predictions about future events (*will*)	
show different degrees of certainty about predictions (*may, might, could*)	
ask and answer questions about future plans and arrangements (*going to*, present continuous)	

Vocabulary

4 Work in pairs. You each get ten seconds to choose a word and name a job that the word describes. Take turns naming jobs with that word and keep going until one person has no more ideas. The other person then gets one point. Repeat with another word. The person with the most points at the end wins.

badly paid	dangerous	glamorous	indoors
manual	outdoors	rewarding	routine

5 Work in pairs. For each of these jobs, discuss what qualities and qualifications you need and what the pay and conditions are like. Then say which job would be best for your partner and give reasons.

accountant	chef	firefighter	pilot	vet

6 Work in groups. Do you agree or disagree with these statements? Why?

1 Everyone should go to college.
2 Failing a test can be a good experience.
3 Dropping out of school is not the end of the world.
4 We never stop learning.

I CAN	
describe different jobs, job requirements, and conditions	
talk about stages in education	

Real life

7 Work in pairs. Match the sentence parts and make requests. Then act out a conversation that includes the requests and appropriate replies.

1 Could you
2 Is it all right if I
3 Would you mind
4 Would it be all right if I

a borrow your phone?
b help me with this application?
c lending me some money?
d took off my jacket?

8 With your partner, act out similar conversations for two of these situations.

a problem at work
a meeting with a new boss
your first day at college

I CAN	
make and respond to requests	

Speaking

9 Work in groups. Each person needs four pieces of paper. Write predictions for these four topics on the pieces of paper. Write two negative and two positive predictions. Put all the pieces of paper together and select them one by one at random. Discuss the probability of the predictions coming true and try to guess who made each one.

entertainment	music	shopping	sports

Tourists take photos of an emperor penguin on the frozen Amundsen Sea in Antarctica.

FEATURES

1 Work in pairs. Look at the photo. Discuss the questions with your partner.

1 What kind of vacation do you think this is? Why?
2 Do you think the people take this kind of trip often? Why?
3 Would you like to take a trip like this?

2 Work in pairs. Which of these travel experiences have you had? Give each other travel tips about them.

being on planes	planning
short business trips	a round-the-world trip
day trips	taking local buses and trains
delays	traveling for work for a week or more
lost luggage	weekends away

3 Which countries or cities have you been to? Find people in your class who have had similar experiences.

Have you been to Russia?

Yes! Have you seen the Kremlin in Moscow?

5a Walking for wildlife

Listening and reading

1 🔊 **16** Look at the map showing the conservationist Mike Fay's trek through central Africa. Choose the options you think are correct. Then listen to part of a radio program and check.

1 The trek covers *almost 2,000 miles / over 3,000 miles*.
2 The route goes through *Kenya / Gabon*.
3 Fay and his companions are *on a walking vacation / working on a project*.
4 The best way to travel in this area is *on foot and by boat / by motorbike and jeep*.
5 It will take *five months / fifteen months* to complete the trek.

2 Read the profile of Mike Fay. Write the number of the paragraph (1–5) next to the heading.

a Has he had any dangerous experiences?
b What has he done?
c What luggage does he usually take?
d Who is he?
e Why does he do it?

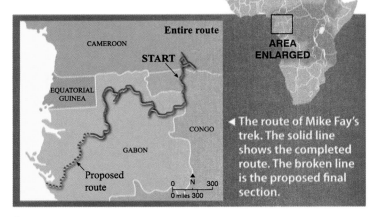

AFRICA

Entire route

CAMEROON

START

EQUATORIAL GUINEA

CONGO

GABON

Proposed route

AREA ENLARGED

◀ The route of Mike Fay's trek. The solid line shows the completed route. The broken line is the proposed final section.

0 N 300
0 miles 300

3 Are the sentences true (T) or false (F)? Test your memory. Then read the profile again and check.

1 He's done conservation work in Africa but not in America.
2 He's slept in 50 different beds in the last ten years.
3 An elephant nearly killed him once.
4 He wore his last pair of sandals for 1,200 miles.
5 He has succeeded in his aims with his work.

4 Work in pairs. Compare Fay's style of traveling with your own. What appeals—or doesn't appeal—to you? Tell your partner.

Walking for wildlife

NATIONAL GEOGRAPHIC PROFILE: MIKE FAY

1 He's a biologist with the Wildlife Conservation Society (WCS). He's lived in central Africa for six years.

2 Fay has worked on several major conservation projects in Africa and America. He's counted all the elephants in the central African country of Chad—twice! He's walked over 1,800 miles across North America. He spends so much time outdoors that he hasn't slept in a bed more than 50 times in the last ten years!

3 A few years ago, he survived a plane crash! And on one trip, he came face to face with a very angry elephant that attacked him. Amazingly, his injuries weren't life-threatening. Less dramatically, but just as seriously, he's had malaria in Africa many times and once he almost died.

4 Fay travels light—he usually just takes a T-shirt, a pair of shorts, and his favorite footwear, sandals. His most recent pair of sandals lasted 1,200 miles before they fell apart! The few items he never travels without include his penknife, a lighter, and a sleeping mat.

5 Fay wants to show people how beautiful and precious the planet is so they will take care of it. And he succeeds. His work has drawn attention to conservation issues and made people act. After he started work on the elephant project in Chad, the number of elephant deaths fell significantly. And in Gabon, the government has created thirteen new national parks covering 10,000 square miles of forest.

trek (n) /trek/ a long, difficult journey, usually on foot

Grammar present perfect and simple past

5 Look at the example. Then read the sentences and choose the correct option.

He's had malaria in Africa many times and once he almost died.

1 We use the *present perfect / simple past* when we don't say exactly when something happened.
2 We use the *present perfect / simple past* when we say—or it is clear from the context—when something happened.

6 Underline the present perfect verbs and circle the simple past verbs in the profile. Which ones have different simple past and past participle forms?

> ▶ **PRESENT PERFECT and SIMPLE PAST**
>
> Present perfect: *He's lived in central Africa for years.*
> Simple past: *A few years ago, he survived a plane crash.*
> Regular verbs: *live, lived, lived*
> Irregular verbs: *have, had, had; come, came, come*
>
> For more information and practice, see page 161.

7 Look at the grammar box. Complete the additional information about Mike Fay with the present perfect and simple past form of the verbs. Then check your answers with your instructor.

> In addition to walking, Fay and his team ¹ _____ (also / fly) over large parts of Africa. Besides his work in Africa, Fay ² _____ (do) extensive conservation work in North America. He ³ _____ (once / spend) 11 months walking the Pacific coast, surveying giant redwood trees. Since he ⁴ _____ (not have) access to electricity for most of that journey, he ⁵ _____ (fill) 24 notebooks with data. He estimates that he ⁶ _____ (use) up hundreds of notebooks over the years.

Pronunciation *has, have*

8 🎧 **17** Listen to these sentences and repeat. Notice the pronunciation of *has* /həz/ and *have* /həv/.

1 The WCS has financed the work.
2 The trip has taken longer than expected.
3 The team members have worked hard.
4 The results have surprised us.
5 The project has been a great success.
6 The government has helped the project.

9 Find these time expressions in the profile. Complete the table with the expressions.

> for   in the last ten years   a few years ago   once

Present perfect	Simple past
already	in 2009
since	last summer
so far	yesterday
this month	

> ▶ **FOR**
>
> We use *for* + period of time with both the present perfect and the simple past.
>
> For more information, see page 162.

10 Complete the sentences so that they are true about you. Then work in pairs and compare your sentences.

1 I've improved my English a lot in the last _____ .
2 I've lived in _____ for _____ .
3 I've _____ many times.
4 I've already _____ this month.
5 I had a great vacation _____ ago.
6 I once worked in a _____ for _____ .
7 I _____ at lunchtime.
8 After I left school, I _____ .

Speaking

11 Have you had any unusual travel experiences? Make as many true or false sentences as you can with these verbs. Then work in pairs and talk about your experiences. Can your partner identify the false sentences? Ask follow-up questions as necessary.

catch	climb	do	fly	go	have
make	meet	run	sail	see	sing
sleep	swim	take	walk		

> *I've flown in a helicopter many times.*

> *Really? I've never done that. Where did you fly to?*

> *I've seen elephants in the wild.*

> *Wow! Did you take any photos?*

5b A good vacation

Vocabulary and reading vacation destinations

1 Which of these words describe the photos (A–D)?

busy street	remote village
crowded market	safe resort
exotic scenery	tropical beach
peaceful setting	unspoiled coastline
relaxing surroundings	vibrant city

2 Work in pairs. Match the features in Exercise 1 with the vacation destinations shown on the map.

3 Read about vacationers. Complete the table with the kinds of vacations for each place.

4 Have you been on any of these kinds of vacations? What is popular in your country?

GEOGRAPHY

Once, a typical vacation was a week at the beach or a lake—near home or somewhere with more reliable weather. But recently, vacationers have been looking for a different vacation experience. Perhaps inspired by wildlife documentaries on television, tourists have been flocking to places like Kenya and South Africa for safaris and bush camps. Interest in China has been growing too. Large numbers of tourists have visited China on cultural tours since the 2008 Olympic Games. Meanwhile, travel companies have been promoting the traditional vacation package with a new twist to attract more customers: spa vacations in Spain and luxury historical tours in Egypt.

One of the most notable changes is that the older generation of vacationers has been traveling like never before. The number of vacationers over 60 has been growing. Cruise destinations in the Caribbean or even to Antarctica are no longer just for young adventurers.

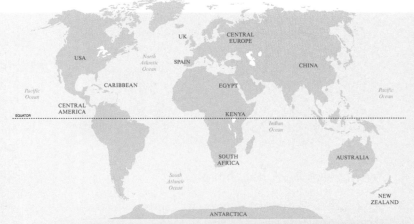

TRAVEL DESTINATIONS AND ACTIVITIES	
Caribbean and Antarctica	1 ....
Kenya and South Africa	2 .... , 3 ....
Spain and Egypt	vacation packages
China	4 ....
US, Australia, and New Zealand	independent travelers, backpackers

Grammar present perfect continuous and present perfect

5 Look at the example. Underline four other present perfect continuous sentences in the text.

> But recently, vacationers have been looking for a different vacation experience.

6 Answer the questions.

1 Which verbs are used to make the present perfect continuous?
2 Do the main verbs describe states or actions?
3 Do the sentences refer to activities that have finished or that are continuing, or both?

▶ **PRESENT PERFECT CONTINUOUS**

subject + *have/has (not) been + -ing*

have/has + subject + *been + -ing*?

For more information and practice, see page 162.

---

7 Compare the present perfect with the present perfect continuous tenses.

1 Which tense emphasizes a completed action?
2 Which tense emphasizes the duration of an activity?
3 Which tense expresses the result of an activity?

8 Match the activities (1–6) with the results (a–f). Then write sentences as in the example.

Example:
1 We've been tracking elephants today—we've taken some amazing photos.

1	track elephants	a	finish my book
2	lie by the pool	b	not find one
3	look for a cheap deal	c	see dozens of churches
4	tour European cities	d	spend a fortune
5	follow the coastal path	e	take amazing photos
6	visit local markets	f	walk ten miles

Listening

9 🔊 **18** Listen to three conversations that Matt has during his vacation. Choose the correct name.

1 *Matt / Li* has been coming here for four years.
2 *Matt / Li* thinks the nightlife is awesome.
3 *Matt / Li* thinks good weather is what you need on vacation.
4 *Matt / Rosa* recommends the food at the SeaView.
5 *Matt / Rosa* wants a relaxing break this year.
6 *Matt / Ping* has good memories of his vacations.
7 *Matt / Ping* has been sky-diving for a long time.
8 *Matt / Ping* spends his vacations with friends.

10 💿 **18** Listen again and complete Matt's questions.

1 How long _____ here?
  About six years.
2 How long _____ here?
  We just got in yesterday.
3 So, how long _____ sky-diving?
  For quite a few years now.
4 How long _____ you?
  It took a while!

Grammar How long... ?

▶ **HOW LONG... ?**

We use *How long... ?* with the present perfect, present perfect continuous, and simple past to ask about the duration of an activity. Verbs like *be, have, know,* and *like* are not usually used in the continuous form.

For more information and practice, see page 162.

---

11 Look at the exchanges in Exercise 10. Which tense is used in the questions—and why?

12 Write questions with *How long... ?* for these sentences. Then work in pairs and continue the conversations.

1 I went to Thailand last year.
2 I'm waiting for the bus to the beach.
3 We're backpacking around India.
4 I'm doing a diving course.
5 We've finally made it home!

Speaking

13 What do you think makes a good vacation? Look at the list and add three ideas of your own.

- getting there: journey time, transportation, _____
- at your destination: things to do, nightlife, beaches, weather, food, friends, _____
- afterwards: good memories, _____

14 Work in pairs. Decide which five things are the most important for a good vacation. Explain your choices with examples from your own vacation experiences.

15 Work with another pair. Compare your ideas. Try to agree on the three most important things. Tell the class.

> *We all agree that good weather is important.*

5c The real cost of travel

Reading

1 What kind of tourism is there in your country or region? List some of the advantages and disadvantages of tourism.

2 Look at the photos in the article on page 63. What aspects of tourism do you think each one shows?

3 Read the article quickly and choose the best option (a–c).

   a It describes how tourists have been getting involved in conservation activities.
   b It compares harmful and beneficial effects of tourism.
   c It looks at the negative impact of tourism.

4 Read the article again and complete the table.

Place	Type of tourism / activity	Effect
Patagonia	1	waste affects 2 ....
Everest	climbing expeditions	the mountain is covered in 3 ....
the Mediterranean	beach resorts	4 .... is out of control
Europe	5	a big impact on 6 ....

5 Answer the questions with information from the article.

   1 Why are cruises bad for the environment?
   2 Expeditions normally climb Everest to reach the top. What other expeditions does the article mention?
   3 Why, aside from the cost, are low-cost flights so popular?
   4 Does the article suggest better ways to travel? How?

Vocabulary conservation

6 Find these words in the article. Then complete the sentences. In one sentence, more than one word is possible.

population	habitats	impact	trash
waste	pollute	greener	

   1 Human activity has a big _____ on wildlife.
   2 On average, each person in the US produces about 1,600 pounds of _____ each year.
   3 The world _____ has doubled since 1960.
   4 We need to protect different natural _____.
   5 Recycling is _____ than throwing things away.
   6 When we fly, we _____ the environment.

Critical thinking close reading

7 Mark these statements true (T), false (F), or not enough information (N) based on the article.

   1 Mass tourism has grown steadily and has now reached its peak.
   2 Cruises have had a negative effect on penguins and other animals.
   3 Non-industrial countries accept the negative effects of tourism.
   4 Economic problems mean that construction on the Mediterranean coast has stopped.
   5 There are less damaging ways of seeing the world than air travel.

8 Discuss the last sentence of the article as a class.

Speaking

9 Work in pairs. Look at these activities and decide their position on the green scale.

   buying out-of-season food flown in from distant destinations
   flying to vacation destinations
   recycling household waste
   saving water
   turning off lights and appliances
   traveling (by bike, car, public transportation)
   upgrading cell phones, computers, and TVs frequently
   using eco-friendly cleaning products

10 How easy is it for you to switch to greener activities? Tell your partner about your experiences with the activities in Exercise 9.

11 Work in groups. Compare your green activities and their results. Is your group "light green" or "dark green"?

This year I've been using a composter. I've reduced my weekly trash to one small bag!

THE REAL COST OF TRAVEL
Mass tourism is a relatively recent phenomenon. The tourism industry took off in the middle of the last century and it's been growing ever since. In the last ten years especially, more and more people have been traveling to places we had previously only read about or seen on television. But what kind of impact does tourism have on the planet?

A VOYAGE TO THE END OF THE EARTH?

A large cruise ship can carry as many as 6,000 passengers and there are upwards of 50 such ships currently sailing the seas. Cruise ships dump about 90,000 tons of waste into the oceans every year. Any harmful effects of this are made even worse by the fact that cruises tend to visit the same places over and over again, thus concentrating the waste in specific places. In Patagonia, this is now having a visible effect on wildlife. The population of animals such as these Magellanic penguins has been in decline for some years now, and things show little sign of changing.

TRASH ON TOP OF THE WORLD

From remote ocean habitats to the world's highest mountain, our trash is everywhere. Despite the fact that far fewer people go climbing or trekking in the Himalayas than on a cruise, their impact is still felt. Tourism is vital to the economy of Nepal, as it is to many non-industrial countries. But for decades, climbers have been abandoning their unwanted equipment on Everest. For the last few years, clean-up teams of local and international climbers have been organizing expeditions just to pick up the waste. One group has brought over eight tons of waste down from the mountain! But their actions don't stop there. The Japanese teams, for example, have also been educating other climbers back home in Japan about being more responsible on the mountain.

WHEN MORE IS NOT BETTER

Tourism of a different kind is causing problems in Europe. Construction on the Mediterranean coast has been spiraling out of control for years. Beach resorts form an almost unbroken line from Gibraltar to Greece, and natural habitats have disappeared under miles of concrete. And so we pollute the sea, the land, and the air. Low-cost air travel is booming, in spite of (or perhaps helped by) economic problems. For many Europeans, low-cost flights allow them to take several short vacations a year. Yet curiously, short flights actually have a much bigger effect on climate change than long-haul flights. So, are there less damaging ways of seeing the world? Traveling by train, for example, is a much greener way of getting around. And many places have been experimenting with low-impact tourism such as ecotourism. It's time to ask ourselves some difficult questions. Have we been destroying the very places we're escaping to?

> **damaging** (adj) /ˈdæmɪdʒɪŋ/ destructive
> **in decline** (adv) /ɪn dɪˈklaɪn/ falling in numbers or quality
> **downside** (n) /ˈdaʊnˌsaɪd/ the negative aspect
> **upwards of** (adv) /ˈʌpwərdz əv/ more than

5d Is something wrong?

Vocabulary travel problems

1 Work in pairs. Have you ever had any travel problems involving these things? Tell your partner. Can a tour guide help you with any of them?

baggage allowances	hotel rooms
boarding passes	infectious diseases
car rental	jetlag
customs	motion sickness
flight delays	passport control
food poisoning	travel documents

> ▶ **WORDBUILDING compound nouns (noun + noun)**
>
> We can use two nouns together to mean one thing.
> *baggage allowances*   *boarding passes*

Real life dealing with problems

2 🎵 **19** Listen to two conversations between a tour guide and tourists. Write the number of the conversation (1–2) next to the problem they talk about. You will only use two options.

a   The person has missed his/her flight home.
b   The luggage hasn't arrived.
c   The flight has been delayed.
d   The person has lost his/her plane tickets.
e   Someone is ill.

3 🎵 **19** Mark each expression for dealing with problems G (guide) or T (tourist) depending on who said it. Then listen again and check.

> ▶ **DEALING WITH PROBLEMS**
>
> I wonder if you could help us?
> Is anything wrong?
> Can I help?
>
> Our luggage hasn't arrived.
> Which flight were you on?
> How did that happen?
> Do you know where our bags have gone to?
> When's the next flight?
> It's about my wife.
> The hotel hasn't provided mosquito nets.
> How long has she been feeling like this?
> Is there anything you can do?
>
> I'm afraid the luggage has gone to Shanghai.
> Don't worry, we'll arrange everything.
> I'll ask the hotel to call a doctor.

4 Work as a class. Are the problems solved? How?

5 **Pronunciation** strong and weak forms

a 🎵 **20** Look at the position of *to* in these sentences. Listen to the sentences. In which sentence is *to* strong—and in which one is it weak?

1   Do you know which airport our bags have gone to?
2   Yes, I'm afraid the luggage has gone to Shanghai.

b 🎵 **21** Listen and repeat these questions. Use strong or weak forms of *at*, *from*, and *for*. Then work in pairs. Ask the questions and give your own answers.

1   Which hotel are you staying at?
2   Are you staying at the Ocean Hotel?
3   Where have you traveled from?
4   Why haven't we heard from the airline?
5   What have we been waiting for?
6   Are you waiting for the manager?

6 Work in pairs. Choose one of the conversations from Exercise 2. Take a role each. Look at the audioscript on page 176 and each take a role. Practice the conversation.

7 Take the roles of a tourist and a tour guide. Choose from the problems in Exercise 2 and act out two conversations. Use the expressions for dealing with problems to help you.

5e Hello from Sydney!

Writing a postcard

Hi!

Greetings from Down Under! Finally made it to Sydney after 18-hour delay in Bangkok!!! Weather here glorious, beaches out of this world, and the people are fantastic. So far have: been surfing (fell off every time!), seen the Opera House (wow!), been on a boat trip around the bay. No kangaroos or koalas yet bc haven't been out of city. Text from my uncle in Brisbane – has found me a job there for the summer!

Lynne

ps new pics up on Flickr®

1 Read the postcard and answer the questions.

1 Where did Lynne come from and where is she now?
2 Who do you think the postcard is to, friends or family?
3 What does Lynne say about the people and places?
4 What has she been doing?

2 Writing skill informal style

a Read the postcard again. Which of these features of informal style does Lynne use?

- abbreviations
- comments in parentheses
- contractions
- exclamation marks
- informal expressions
- listing items
- leaving out words

b Look at the example. The words *I* and *an* are missing. Mark their position in the complete sentence.

Finally made it to Sydney after 18-hour delay in Bangkok!

c Mark the places in the postcard where Lynne has omitted words. What are the words?

d Rewrite the sentences. Omit words where possible.

1 The weather is sunny and it has been very hot.
2 I've been touring all the typical places— it's exhausting!
3 The people here are very kind and they have helped me a lot.
4 I took some photos of some koalas— they're so cute!
5 I haven't heard anything from Suri yet.
6 I'm taking a bus up to Brisbane because flying is too expensive.

3 Choose a place you have visited and make notes about it. Use the questions in Exercise 1 as a guide.

4 Write a postcard of about 100 words describing your trip. Use some of the features of informal style from Exercise 2 and omit unecessary words.

5 Send your postcard to someone in your class. Then read the postcard you have received. Use these questions to check your classmate's postcard.

- Is everything clearly expressed?
- Are there any sections you do not understand?

6 Work in pairs. Tell your partner about the postcard you have received.

I got a postcard from Daisuke the other day.

Oh, yeah! How's he doing?

A disappearing world

It's an amazing place!

Before you watch

1 Work in pairs. Look at the title of this video and the photo and discuss the questions.

1 What do you think this video is about?
2 Which parts of the world have rain forests?
3 What do you know about the rain forest and its problems?

2 Write down four animals and birds you think you will see in the video.

While you watch

3 Watch the video and check your answers from Exercises 1 and 2.

4 Put the events in the order you see them in the video.

a looking over treetops
b writing a journal
c filming an elephant
d reaching the sea
e climbing a hill
f crossing rapids
g traveling in a canoe

5 Watch the video again. What does this information refer to?

1 September ....
2 1200 ....
3 5800 ....
4 one quarter ....
5 half ....
6 eight ....
7 70 or 80 ....
8 360 ....
9 six hundred ....
10 fifteen ....

6 Complete the sentences with words from the glossary.

1 Their .... is to make a scientific .... of a world that could be disappearing from Earth.
2 What I'm trying to do, in a .... way, is to show the world that we're just about to lose the last little .... in the African continent.
3 Fay's plan is to .... and record data on almost every part of the rain forest.
4 Their next .... is to reach a group of strange hills that are made of stone, and that .... far above the forest floor.
5 This land of fast water and old forests is in danger because of ....

After you watch

7 **Roleplay an interview with an expedition member**

Work in pairs.

Student A: You are a writer for National Geographic. You are going to interview a member of Michael Fay's team. Use the ideas below to prepare questions.

Student B: You have just completed the Congo Basin "Megatransect" with Michael Fay. Use the ideas below to prepare what you are going to say to the interviewer.

- purpose of the expedition
- how you traveled
- what you saw
- the most difficult parts
- the best parts
- dangerous experiences

Act out the interview. Then change roles and repeat the interview.

8 During the video, Dr. Fay says: "If we don't do something now, if we don't do it today, we can forget about it." What does he mean?

9 Work in pairs. Discuss these questions.

1 What do you think Dr. Fay did with the information he collected during his expedition?
2 Apart from logging, what other dangers do places like the Congo Basin face?
3 Are you optimistic or pessimistic about whether we will be able to preserve wild places on our planet?

aim (n) /eɪm/ objective
challenge (n) /ˈtʃælɪndʒ/ something that tests a person's abilities
collect (v) /kəˈlekt/ pick up or bring things together
desperate (adj) /ˈdespərɪt/ needing to change a very bad situation
gem (n) /dʒem/ something very valuable
logging (n) /ˈlɑgɪŋ/ cutting down trees on a large scale
overwhelmed (adj) /ˌoʊvərˈwelmd/ feeling very emotional
rapids (n) /ˈræpɪdz/ part of a river where the water flows very fast, usually over and between rocks
record (n) /ˈrekərd/ written information about something
rise (v) /raɪz/ go up
stepping stones (n) /ˈstepɪŋ ˌstoʊnz/ large stones that people walk on to cross a river

UNIT 5 REVIEW

Grammar

1 Work in pairs. Look at the photo. Discuss the questions.

1 Where do wild gorillas live?
2 What are the problems facing gorillas in the wild?
3 Have you heard any news stories about gorillas?

2 Read the article and check your ideas from Exercise 1. Then choose the correct option.

Wild gorillas [1] *faced / have faced* many challenges in recent years. Commercial hunters [2] *left / have been leaving* several young mountain gorillas orphaned, and the Ebola virus [3] *devastated / has devastated* the population of lowland gorillas. Gorilla numbers [4] *declined / have declined* at a disturbing rate—down over 50 percent since the 1990s. In 2007, their status [5] *changed / has changed* from endangered to critically endangered. Projects such as the *Project Protection des Gorilles* [6] *rescued / have rescued* young gorillas and they [7] *have encouraged / have been encouraging* them to form new social groups, hoping to give them a second chance in the wild. Meanwhile, to counter the threat of the Ebola virus, Peter Walsh and others [8] *have worked / have been working* on a vaccine that will prevent the transmission of the virus among gorillas.

3 Have you ever been to any of these places? Ask your partner questions about their experience.

| a safari park | a wildlife sanctuary | a zoo |

I CAN	
talk about recent activities and experiences (present perfect and continuous)	
relate events that happened at a specific time in the past (simple past)	

Vocabulary

4 Work in pairs. Which is the odd one out in each group? Why?

1 exotic, plane, peaceful, vibrant
2 cruise, peaceful, package, safari
3 fly, food, nightlife, weather
4 litter, trash, ticket, waste
5 journey, ocean, tour, trip

5 Work in groups. Discuss the questions.

1 Where do tourists go in your country?
2 What have you done to help the environment?
3 Where did you go for your last vacation? What did you do there?

I CAN	
describe vacation destinations	
talk about conservation	
talk about vacations	

Real life

6 Read these sentences from a conversation between two friends. Put the sentences (a–h) in order (1–8).

a A: What? How did that happen?
b A: Well, let's take another look. Calm down.
c A: Have you looked in all your pockets?
d A: Is anything wrong?   *1*
e B: Yes, I have. And I've checked the suitcase.
f B: I've been worrying so much about everything, and now this!
g B: I think I've lost the boarding passes.
h B: I don't know. I thought they were with my passport, but they aren't there now.

7 Act out similar conversations in pairs.

Conversation 1: Student A is a tourist and Student B is a tour guide. Student A has lost his/her passport.

Conversation 2: Student A is an airline official and Student B is a customer. The flight is canceled.

I CAN	
talk about travel problems	
ask for and give explanations	

Speaking

8 Prepare questions to interview someone about their career. Use the ideas below. Then work in pairs and choose a role on page 155.

How long / be a... ?	Where / travel to?
What / do / recently?	When / go to... ?
Have / unusual experiences?	

9 Work with a new partner. Take turns asking and answering your questions.

How long have you been a pilot?

Food items from the Overall Nutritional Quality Index, which assesses the nutritional value of food
Photograph by Mark Thiessen

FEATURES

1 Find these foods in the photo. Which ones do you eat? How often do you eat them?

avocado	bagel	cheese	cheese snacks	chocolate
fried egg	pasta	peanuts	popcorn	shrimp steak

2 Work in pairs. Put the foods in Exercise 1 in the order you think is the most (1) to the least (11) healthy.

3 Answer the questions.

1 Should supermarkets be required to tell you how nutritious the food on their shelves is?
2 Should restaurants provide nutritional information on their menus?
3 Where can you already find this kind of information?

4 Discuss the questions with your partner.

1 Have you heard the saying "You are what you eat"? Do you have a similar saying in your country?
2 How much attention do you pay to your diet?
3 In what ways can food and diet influence your health?

6a Pizza with a pedigree

Reading

1 Work in pairs. Answer the questions.

1 What are the traditional dishes of your country or region?
2 How often do you eat or make them?
3 How often do you eat or make dishes from other countries? Which dishes?

2 Read the text and answer the questions.

1 Why is Pizza Napoletana in the news?
2 What are some of the other foods in the same group as Pizza Napoletana?
3 Which aspects of "authentic" Pizza Napoletana are regulated?

3 Which food and drink products have protected status in your country?

Grammar modal verbs (1)

<table>
<tr><td colspan="2">▶ MODAL VERBS</td></tr>
<tr><td colspan="2">Obligation or no obligation</td></tr>
<tr><td>+ have to / has to, must</td><td>– don't/doesn't have to</td></tr>
<tr><td colspan="2">Prohibition</td></tr>
<tr><td></td><td>– can't</td></tr>
<tr><td colspan="2">Permission or no permission/prohibition</td></tr>
<tr><td>+ can, is/are allowed to</td><td>– can't, is/are not allowed to</td></tr>
<tr><td colspan="2">Recommendation</td></tr>
<tr><td></td><td>should (not)</td></tr>
</table>

The modal *mustn't* is used less frequently in American English than it is in British English. In American English, *must not* or *can't* are more common. For more information and practice, see page 163.

4 Look at the grammar box.

1 Underline the modal verbs in the news item.
2 The modal verbs *have to* and *must* have the same form in the simple past. What is it?
3 Two of the modal verbs in the news item do not express rules. Which verbs?

F O O D

Pizza with a pedigree

There is pizza—and there is Pizza Napoletana. The two, connoisseurs say, have as much in common as virgin olive oil has with generic cooking oil. Now, authentic Pizza Napoletana has joined the elite group of European-Union-certified food and drink products—like Scottish Farmed Salmon, Spanish Melon from La Mancha, and English Blue Stilton cheese—that have to meet very strict criteria.

Once a product is granted Guaranteed Traditional Specialty status, other similar products are not allowed to use the same name. If your champagne doesn't come from that particular region of France, for example, you can't call it champagne. But be warned: it takes longer to read the EU specifications for "real" Pizza Napoletana than it does to make one. To be labeled "Guaranteed Traditional Speciality," the pizza can't be over 14 inches in diameter and the crust can't be more than three-quarters of an inch thick. The ingredients must include type 00 flour and up to three and a half ounces of San Marzano tomatoes applied in a spiraling motion. And the cheese has to be fresh "Mozzarella di Bufala."

Pizza has a long history in Italy. The word first appeared in a 997 CE manuscript from Gaeta, a southern Italian town. A millennium later, in 1997, political groups in northern Italy tried to boycott pizza because it was a symbol of their rivals in the south. Perhaps they should accept that Pizza Napoletana is here to stay now. Thankfully, you don't have to know anything about history to enjoy an authentic Pizza Napoletana!

elite (adj) (n) /ɪˈlit/ a small group of the best
(be) granted (v) /ˈɡræntɪd/ (be) officially given, awarded
pedigree (n) (adj) /ˈpedɪˌɡri/ a documented history
strict (adj) /strɪkt/ precise and rigorous

5 Read the labels from food packaging. Look at the example. Then write sentences using one of the modal verbs in parentheses.

Suitable for vegetarians

1
(can / don't have to)
Example:
Vegetarians can eat this product.

**NOT SUITABLE FOR PEOPLE
WITH NUT ALLERGIES**

2
(don't have to / shouldn't)

**DO NOT EXCEED THE RECOMMENDED
DAILY INTAKE OF SALT**

3
(can / shouldn't)

SAMPLE – NOT FOR SALE

4
(don't have to / not allowed to)

Heat thoroughly before serving

5
(can / have to)

**NOT RECOMMENDED FOR
DIABETICS**

6
(allowed to / shouldn't)

6 Work in pairs. Look at these food items. Answer the questions.

durian	eggs	fugu	hakarl
oysters	potatoes	red beans	steak

1 Which of these food items have you eaten?
2 Do you know of any special treatment these things need before you can eat them?

7 🔊 **22** Listen to the conversations about the food items in Exercise 6 and check your ideas. Complete the notes.

1 durian: you're not allowed to _____
2 eggs: you should _____
3 fugu: _____ are allowed to _____
4 hakarl: you have to _____
5 oysters: you can't _____
6 potatoes: you don't have to _____
7 red beans: must _____
8 steak: you can _____

> **ferment** (v) /fərˈment/ to let food or drink undergo a natural chemical reaction
> **peel** (v) /piːl/ to remove the skin from fruits or vegetables
> **raw** (adj) /rɔː/ uncooked or not well-cooked

8 Pronunciation weak forms

a 🔊 **23** Listen to some of the information from the conversations in Exercise 7. Notice how *to* is not stressed. Repeat the sentences.

b Work in pairs. Decide if you (don't) have to do these things. Discuss with your partner.

> keep eggs in the fridge
> wash rice before you cook it
> eat fish on the day you buy it
> cook meat until it isn't pink

Speaking

9 Work in pairs. Choose a dish you both like. Do you agree on the following points? Make notes using modal verbs where necessary. Then tell the class about the dish.

- essential ingredients
- optional ingredients
- cooking method
- presentation
- when and where to eat the dish

> *We'd like to tell you the secret of a good paella.*

> *You can make it with seafood or meat, but we think it's better with seafood.*

fugu (puffer fish)

a durian

hakarl (shark meat)

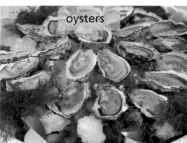
oysters

6b Imaginary eating

Reading and listening

1 Work in pairs. Discuss the statements. Do you agree with them?

1 Self-confidence: the difference between a winner and a runner-up is in attitude, not skill.
2 Willpower: you can achieve anything if you think you can do it.
3 Train your mind: people who consider themselves to be lucky have more "lucky" moments.

2 Read the news item *Imaginary eating*. What does the imaginary eating technique consist of?

3 🔊 **24** Listen to two people discussing the news item. Are these sentences true (T) or false (F)?

1 Jack doesn't believe the claims in the news item but Lin does.
2 Lin is open-minded about the idea.
3 Both of them agree that willpower is important.
4 Lin thinks Jack should try out the technique.
5 Lin eats too many snacks.
6 Jack is going to buy some chocolate.

4 🔊 **24** Listen to the conversation again. Match the two parts of the sentences.

1 I'll believe it
2 If you don't train your mind,
3 I won't find out
4 When I want to eat a snack,
5 I'll never have to buy chocolate again
6 As soon as it starts working,

a if this technique works.
b I'll let you know.
c I'll try just imagining it.
d unless I try.
e when I see it.
f you won't be able to lose weight.

5 Read the comment at the end of the news item again. Do you agree with it? With your partner, write your own comment to add to the comments section.

Imaginary eating

Christine Dell'Amore
National Geographic News
December 9

Obesity rates are climbing fast and we need to find new techniques for controlling overeating. According to new research, "imaginary eating" could be one such technique. A psychologist in the US reports that if you imagine eating a specific food, your interest in that food will drop. And if you are less interested in that food, you'll eat less of it. Carey Morewedge explains that people often try to avoid thinking about food when they need to lose weight. However, this might not, in fact, be a good strategy. On the other hand, if you force yourself to think about chewing and actually swallowing food, you'll reduce your craving.

COMMENTS

Rpineapple23 *11:09 a.m. on December 12*
This study is more proof of how powerful our brain is. The better we are at using that power when making decisions and controlling certain behaviors (such as food cravings), the healthier we will become.

(reply)   (recommend)

craving (n) /ˈkreɪvɪŋ/ a strong feeling that you want or need something

Grammar first conditional

6 Look at these sentences and answer the questions.

   a I'll never have to buy chocolate again if this technique works.

   b If you don't train your mind, you won't be able to lose weight.

   1 Which tenses are used to make the first conditional?

   2 Where can *if* go in conditional sentences?

   3 Look at the position of *if* in the sentences. When do we use a comma (,)?

   4 Do the sentences refer to the past, the present, or the future? (More than one option is possible.)

   5 Find three sentences in the news item that use the first conditional pattern. Do the sentences refer to future possibilities or things that are generally true?

► FIRST CONDITIONAL		
If + simple present	,	*will* + infinitive
will + infinitive		*if* + simple present
For more information and practice, see page 164.		

7 Look at the grammar box. Complete the sentences with the simple present and *will* + infinitive.

   1 If you _____ (believe) in yourself, you _____ (be) more successful.

   2 I _____ (need) a lot of willpower if I _____ (want) to give up chocolate.

   3 If you _____ (not buy) snacks, you _____ (not be able) to eat them.

   4 If you _____ (find) any more information, _____ (you / let) me know?

   5 If we _____ (go) to the supermarket, we _____ (check) the price.

   6 I _____ (give up) junk food if you _____ (do) too.

   7 If I _____ (not try) it, I _____ (never know).

   8 What _____ (you / do) if your plan _____ (not work)?

► *WHEN, AS SOON AS, UNLESS, UNTIL, BEFORE*
We use the present tense after these words when we refer to future events.
For more information and practice, see page 164.

8 Read the sentences and cross out any options that are not possible. In some cases, both answers are possible.

   1 You won't change *as soon as / unless* you make an effort.

   2 *As soon as / When* you make up your mind, you'll be able to act.

   3 I'll weigh myself *before / when* I start my diet.

   4 I'll keep trying *before / until* I see a change.

   5 You won't see any results *unless / when* you try hard.

   6 *If / Unless* you give up easily, you won't achieve your target.

   7 *If / When* you are ready to try, I'll be happy to help.

   8 It will be a while *before / until* you notice a difference.

Vocabulary and speaking a healthy lifestyle

9 Work in pairs. Match the verbs with the nouns to make strategies for a healthy lifestyle. You can match some verbs with more than one noun and some nouns with more than one verb. Add ideas of your own.

Verbs	Nouns
avoid	a new sport
change	an outdoor activity
cut down on	bad habits
cut out	computer and TV time
give up	fatty food
learn	heavy meals at night
reduce	junk food
take up	relaxation techniques
	smoking
	snacks between meals
	stress

► WORDBUILDING phrasal verbs
Phrasal verbs with *down* and *up* often describe change.
cut down   *give up*

10 Think of a specific result for each strategy from Exercise 9. Write sentences with the first conditional.

Example:
If you avoid heavy meals at night, you'll sleep better.

11 Work with a new partner. Act out two conversations. Try to motivate your partner.

Student A: You've been told to change to a healthier diet.

Student B: You've been told you spend too much time sitting around and need to get more exercise.

> *I have to change my diet, but I don't want to give up my favorite foods!*

> *You could try imaginary eating.*

6c A caffeine-fueled world

Reading

1 Work in groups. Discuss your answers to these questions.

1 Is your lifestyle very different from that of your parents' generation? In what way(s)?
2 What kind of comments do people in your age group make about work, relationships, time, and modern life?
3 How much tea, coffee, or other beverages do you drink in a normal day?

2 Read the article on page 75 and choose the correct option.

The article is about caffeine and *children / daily life / science.*

3 Complete these sentences.

1 Tea, coffee, soft drinks, energy drinks, and _____ are all sources of caffeine.
2 Caffeine is classified as a psychoactive _____ .
3 In Europe, there are various regulations on the sale of _____ drinks.
4 Modern lifestyles depend on caffeinated _____ and _____ .
5 Caffeine changes the natural _____ of the human body.

4 What are the effects of caffeine? Complete the table.

Beneficial effects of caffeine
makes you less tired
makes you _____
relieves _____
reduces asthma _____
increases _____

Harmful effects of caffeine
is mood-altering
is _____
raises _____
increases the _____ of heart disease

5 Answer the questions based on the article.

1 How have people's working patterns changed?
2 What helped us adapt to those changes?
3 What are the risks of not getting enough sleep?
4 What is the caffeine paradox?

6 Work in pairs. Did any of the information about caffeine surprise you? Tell your partner.

Critical thinking language clues

7 Find words in the article that signal the following.

1 introducing a contrasting idea (paragraph 2):
_____ , _____ , _____
2 introducing a consequence:
_____ , _____ (paragraph 2)
_____ , _____ (paragraph 3)

8 Identify the two contrasting ideas for each of the words from Exercise 7 item 1.

9 Work in pairs. Discuss the questions.

1 Do you think caffeine is harmful, beneficial, neither, or both?
2 Did you change your ideas about caffeine after reading the article?

Vocabulary and speaking modern life

10 Which things are typical of a 24-hour society?

daylight work schedules	indoor jobs
electric light	living by the clock
heart disease	a natural sleep cycle
high blood pressure	tiredness

11 Complete the slogans about modern life with these words. Where do you think the slogans are from?

all   close   day   night   on   today

1 We never _____ .
2 See the movies of tomorrow _____ .
3 Open _____ hours.
4 All _____ breakfast served here.
5 Late _____ shopping every Thursday.
6 "Always _____" broadband.

12 Work in pairs. Make notes about modern life under two headings: *good things* and *bad things*. You can use ideas from Exercise 10. Then work in groups and discuss how the pace of modern life affects you.

> *I'm lucky because I don't have to live by the clock at the moment. I suppose that will change when I start working full-time.*

> *Yes, it will! My problem is working under electric lights all day. It really makes me tired.*

> *Me too.*

A *caffeine*
-fueled world

Over the centuries, people have created many rituals to accompany the consumption of their favorite drinks, tea and coffee. Just think of the Japanese tea ceremony, British afternoon tea, or the morning coffee and coffee break ritual in countless societies. Why are these drinks so popular? The answer is their secret ingredient: caffeine. In the modern world, the new caffeine "delivery systems" are canned "energy" drinks. And the more modern our world gets, the more we seem to need caffeine. People have known for years that caffeinated drinks make you less tired and more alert. This dual power of caffeine to counteract physical fatigue and increase alertness is part of the reason why it is the world's most popular mood-altering drug. It is the only habit-forming psychoactive drug we routinely serve to our children (in all those soft drinks and chocolate bars). In fact, most babies in the developed world are born with traces of caffeine in their bodies.

Most people don't think twice about their caffeine intake. However, caffeine raises blood pressure and thus increases the risk of heart disease. The widespread use of caffeine is now a cause for concern among scientists and public health officials. One result of this concern is that you are not allowed to sell energy drinks in France or Denmark. And in other European countries, manufacturers have to label cans with warnings.

The United States has no such rule, but many canned energy drinks sold there carry warnings anyway. On the other hand, much of the research suggests that caffeine may have health benefits. Studies have shown it helps relieve pain, reduces asthma symptoms, and increases reaction speed. Despite this, a study in Ireland recommended that children and pregnant women, among other groups, shouldn't drink energy drinks.

But we need coffee—or Diet Coke® or Red Bull—to get us out of bed and back to work. "For most of human existence, the pattern of sleeping and waking has followed sunrise and sunset," explains Charles Czeisler, a neuroscientist at Harvard Medical School. "Then, the way we work changed from a schedule built around the sun to an indoor job timed by a clock, and consequently humans had to adapt. Electric light and caffeinated food and drinks allowed people to follow a work schedule set by the clock, not by daylight or the natural sleep cycle." Therefore, without caffeine, the 24-hour society of the developed world simply couldn't exist.

"Caffeine helps people try to override the human rhythm that is in all of us," says Czeisler. "Nevertheless," he says solemnly, "there is a heavy, heavy price to pay for all this extra wakefulness." Without adequate sleep—the conventional eight hours out of each 24 is about right—the human body will not function at its best physically, mentally, or emotionally.

But our caffeine use has created a downward spiral. People need caffeine to stay awake, but as Czeisler points out, "the main reason they can't stay awake is they don't get enough regular sleep—because they use caffeine."

---

counteract (v) /ˌkaʊntərˈækt/ to reduce the effect of something by acting against it
fatigue (n) /fəˈtig/ the feeling of being extremely tired
traces (n) /ˈtreɪsɪz/ very small amounts of something

6d Eating out

Vocabulary restaurants

1 Work in pairs. Which are the most important things to consider when eating out? Does it depend on the occasion?

> the atmosphere in the restaurant
> the food choice and/or quality
> the prices and/or value for money
> the service

2 Put these stages in eating out (a–h) in order (1–8).

a make a
   reservation   *1*
b have an appetizer
c have dessert
d have an entree

e leave a tip
f look at the menu
g order something to
   drink
h pay the bill

3 Are these comments usually said by a customer (C), a waiter (W), or both (B)?

1 Are you ready to order?
2 Would you like something to drink while you decide?
3 What's that made from?
4 What do they taste like?
5 I think I'll try that.
6 Can I take your order now?
7 And I'll have the same.
8 And for your entree?
9 Does it come with vegetables?
10 And what about you, sir?
11 Certainly.

Real life describing dishes

4 🔊 **25** Listen to the conversation in a Jamaican restaurant. Check your answers from Exercise 3.

5 🔊 **25** Look at the expressions for describing dishes. Listen to the conversation again. How are the dishes in the photos described?

> ▶ **DESCRIBING DISHES**
>
> It's / They're a sort / type / kind of:
> *baked / boiled / fried dish /*
> *fruit / meat / fish / vegetable*
>
> It's / They're made from:
> *a kind of bean / meat / vegetables*
>
> It tastes / They taste:
> *bland / hot / salty / spicy / sweet*
>
> It's / They're a bit like:
> *fresh cod / potatoes / lamb*

6 🔊 **25** Which of the four dishes do the customers order? Listen to the conversation again and check your answers. Would you order the same?

Diner 1	Diner 2

7 Write a list of six dishes, vegetables, fruit, or other food that are either from your country or that you have eaten abroad. Make notes that describe each item. Use the expressions for describing dishes to help you.

Food	Taste

8 Work in groups of three. Take turns describing and guessing your mystery foods.

plantain fritters

akkra

ackee and saltfish

goat curry

6e A staff meeting

Writing a formal letter

1 The employees at a small company, Hardwick Health Solutions, have written to the owner. Read the letter quickly. What is its purpose? Choose the correct option (a–c).

a to accept a proposal
b to make a proposal
c to object to a proposal

Dear Mrs. Hardwick,

We are writing to express our concern at the plan to close the staff restaurant at the end of this month.

In our view, this action will have serious consequences for all the staff. If there is no on-site restaurant, employees will have to travel to the nearest town at lunchtime. This could lead to time-management and punctuality issues.

In addition, it is important for working people to eat a healthy meal at lunchtime. If the restaurant closes, this will result in many people eating snacks and sandwiches. This kind of food is not nutritious and therefore staff health and productivity could suffer.

Currently, the staff are not allowed to eat at their workstations. How will the closure of the restaurant affect this policy? Will there be plans for a kitchen or food area?

We request a meeting to discuss these issues at your earliest convenience.

Yours sincerely,

PJ Firth

PJ Firth
Staff Representative

2 Answer the questions about each paragraph.

Paragraph 1: What is the proposal?
Paragraph 2: What consequences of this plan are mentioned?
Paragraph 3: What additional consequences of the plan are mentioned?
Paragraph 4: What questions does the writer have?
Paragraph 5: What does the writer want to happen next?

3 Writing skill explaining consequences

a Find these words in the letter. They link causes and consequences. For each word, underline the cause and circle the consequence in the letter.

1 lead to (paragraph 2)
2 result in (paragraph 3)
3 therefore (paragraph 3)

b Complete the sentences with these words. Sometimes, more than one option is possible.

consequently   lead to   means   result in   so
therefore   thus

1 We object strongly to this proposal.
_____ , we will not be able to support it.
2 We welcome the new staff kitchen. This will _____ more people eating a hot meal.
3 The menu prices have gone up. _____ , fewer people will continue to eat in the cafeteria.
4 A new take-out place in this area _____ we'll have more choice.
5 We suggest changing the menu since this could _____ more customers coming in.
6 We reduced our prices and _____ increased the number of customers.

4 Prepare a letter supporting or objecting to one of these proposals. Make notes before you start. Use the questions in Exercise 2 to guide you.

- Your college is going to close the student cafeteria.
- A late-night take-out restaurant is going to open on your street.
- Your employer is going to ban food and drink in the workplace.
- Your college or workplace is going to install vending machines with healthy snacks only.

5 Write your letter. Follow the structure of the paragraphs in Exercise 2. Use these questions to check your letter.

- Is the style correct for a formal letter?
- Is the purpose of the letter clear?
- Is it clear what action you are recommending?

6 Exchange letters with your partner. Read your partner's letter. Take the role of the person it is addressed to. Are you going to take any action as a result of the letter? Write a short reply.

Eating this fish is like playing a dangerous game.

Before you watch

1 Work in groups. Look at the photo and discuss the questions.

1 Where was the photo taken?
2 Would you eat this fish in a restaurant?
3 What does the caption suggest about the fish?

2 Mark the things you think you will see people doing in this video.

> buying fish   catching fish   cooking fish
> cutting fish   eating fish

While you watch

3 Watch the video and check your answers from Exercise 2.

4 Watch the first part of the video (to 02:49). Are these sentences true (T) or false (F)? Correct the false sentences.

1 Puffer fish is very cheap.
2 All restaurants in Tokyo serve fugu.
3 Puffer fish toxin is 100 times stronger than cyanide.
4 Chef Hayashi has a lot of experience preparing fugu.
5 You have to have a special license to cook fugu in Japan.
6 Between 1945 and 1975, 2,500 Japanese people died from eating fugu.
7 Nobody dies from fugu poisoning any more.
8 Most poisonings happen after people eat fugu in restaurants.

5 Watch the second part of the video (02:52 to the end) and answer the questions. Then compare your answers with a partner.

1 What does Yuji Nagashima study? What does he hope to develop?
2 How much of the toxin is enough to kill a person? What are the effects of the toxin?
3 What treatment should a person who has eaten puffer fish poison receive?
4 How much of the puffer fish does Chef Hayashi throw away? Which two parts does he say are poisonous?

6 Complete the information about Tom Caradonna. Then watch the whole video again and check your answers.

Tom has decided to eat [1] _____ in the famous Matsumoto restaurant in Tokyo. The restaurant is [2] _____ years old. Tom has heard stories about people [3] _____ when they eat fugu, but he is not worried. Chef Hayasahi tells Tom and Aki that everything will be [4] _____ . He shows them his fugu chef's [5] _____ . The meal that Tom and Aki eat has [6] _____ different dishes, and includes sake topped with a cooked fugu [7] _____ . During the meal, Tom laughs and says that he can still [8] _____ !

After you watch

7 **Roleplay** an interview in a fugu restaurant

Work in pairs.

Student A: A friend has invited you to eat in a fugu restaurant, but you are a little worried. Use the ideas below to prepare questions you want to ask the chef.

Student B: You are a chef in a fugu restaurant. Use the ideas below to prepare what you are going to say to a worried customer.

• chef's qualifications to prepare fugu
• how long chef has worked with fugu
• which parts are dangerous
• how much of the fish is dangerous
• what happens if you eat the poison
• what the restaurant does in an emergency

Act out the interview. Then change roles and act out the interview again. Do you want to eat fugu in this restaurant?

8 Work in groups. Discuss these questions.

1 What traditional dishes do people like to eat in your country?
2 Are any of these dishes dangerous or unusual?
3 Do you think it is important to maintain the traditional dishes of a country?

---

concern (v) /kənˈsɜrn/ worry
cute (adj) /kjut/ attractive
cyanide (n) /ˈsaɪəˌnaɪd/ a type of poison
fin (n) /fɪn/ a thin triangular part of a fish's body that helps it to swim
fool (v) /ful/ make someone believe something that is not true
funeral (n) /ˈfjunərəl/ a ceremony for a dead person
gill (n) /gɪl/ the part of its body that a fish uses to breathe
paralyze (v) /ˈpærəˌlaɪz/ make something stop moving

poison (n) /ˈpɔɪzən/ a substance that can kill people if they eat it
poison (v) /ˈpɔɪzən/ kill or make a person sick with poison
puffer fish (n) /ˈpʌfər ˌfɪʃ/ a type of fish that can fill its body with air
regulations (n) /ˌregjəˈleɪʃənz/ official controls
sake (n) /ˈsɑki/ Japanese rice wine
toxin (n) /ˈtɑksɪn/ poison
wear off (v) /ˈwear ˈɔf/ stop having an effect

UNIT 6 REVIEW

Grammar

1 Read the conversation between two friends who are cooking. Cross out the incorrect options.

A: Do you know how to make risotto?
B: Oh yes. I ¹ *show / will show* you if you want.
A: OK, great. Well, I think I've got everything I need. ² *Can / Must* I use this pan?
B: Yes, sure. You ³ *have to / don't have to* ask.
A: When the onion ⁴ *is / will be* ready, I add the rice.
B: Yes, then the liquid. But you ⁵ *must / have to* add it slowly. Don't add more until the rice ⁶ *absorbs / will absorb* it.
A: ⁷ *Am I allowed to / Should* I stir it all the time?
B: Yes, because if it ⁸ *sticks / will stick*, it will burn.
A: ⁹ *Should I / Do I have to* add salt?
B: You can if you want to, but you ¹⁰ *can't / don't have to*. And the risotto ¹¹ *can't / has to* rest for a while before you ¹² *eat / will eat* it.
A: ¹³ *Am I allowed to / Do I have to* taste it?
B: Of course you are. You made it!

2 Work in pairs. Check your answers from Exercise 1.

3 Work in pairs. Take turns to state an intention and start a "chain." Follow the example below. How many results can you give?

give up / start eating meat	open a restaurant
give up / start smoking	sell my car
join a gym	take a vacation

> *I think I'll go on a diet.*

> *If you go on a diet, you'll lose weight.*

> *If I lose weight, I'll have to buy new clothes.*

I CAN	
talk about obligation, prohibition, permission, and recommendation (modal verbs)	☐
talk about the future results of present and future actions (first conditional)	☐

4 Which three pairs of verbs have the same meanings?

cut down on	cut out	give up
learn	reduce	take up

5 Work in groups. Discuss the connections between these pairs of things and how people can avoid the health problems. Use the verbs from Exercise 4.

1 fatty food + heart disease
2 junk food + high blood pressure
3 living by the clock + stress
4 bad habits + tiredness

Vocabulary

6 Work in pairs. Tell your partner if you never, always, or sometimes do these things when you eat out. Explain your reasons.

make a reservation	leave a tip
have an appetizer	look at the menu
have dessert	order a drink
have an entree	pay the bill

I CAN	
describe different foods	☐
talk about healthy living and modern lifestyles	☐
order food in a restaurant	☐

Real life

7 Look at the photo and choose the correct caption (a–b).

a Sushi is a Japanese dish. It's a type of seafood dish, made with balls or squares of rice, seaweed, and raw fish.
b Ceviche is a Latin American dish. It's also a seafood dish, made by using the juice of citrus, in this case limes, to "cook" a mixture of raw fish and seafood.

8 Work in groups. Prepare descriptions of as many dishes from the list as you can.

baklava	borscht	wontons	couscous	
fondue	pad thai	gravlax	kebab	lasagna
paella	pizza	risotto	curry	tortilla

9 Compare your descriptions with other groups. Are there any dishes nobody is familiar with? Look at page 155 to find out what they are.

I CAN	
ask about and describe different dishes	☐

Speaking

10 Work in groups. Discuss the rules your parents set for meal times when you were growing up. Was/ Is it the same for all the family? Are/Will you be the same with your own children?

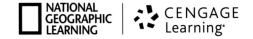

4a
Combo Split
Workbook

Paul Dummett
John Hughes
Helen Stephenson

Contents

Unit 1 Color

1a Red alert!

Grammar simple present and present continuous

1 Complete the sentences with the simple present or present continuous form of the verbs.

1 People _____ (spend) over a hundred million dollars every year on red hair dye.

2 It _____ (seem) that a lot of us _____ (like) red.

3 Natural redheads aren't very common—they _____ (belong) to a minority.

4 In Scotland two out of five people _____ (possess) the gene for red hair.

5 Some redheads _____ (feel) the cold more.

6 You _____ (need) two copies of the gene to get red hair.

7 That's why natural redheads _____ (disappear).

8 Young people often _____ (move) away from their home areas to work or to study.

9 The chances of someone meeting another person with the red-hair gene _____ (get) smaller.

10 Now some scientists _____ (speculate) that by the year 2100 true redheads will be extinct.

2 Look at the sentences in Exercise 1. Find words with the opposite meaning to these words.

1 artificial: _____
2 rare: _____
3 majority: _____
4 the heat: _____
5 greater: _____

3 Read the article about dyes. Complete the article with the simple present and present continuous form of these verbs.

| become | cause | come | contain | increase |
| know | not / understand | now / report | use | |

W e [1] _____ dyes to change the color of or add color to many things. Textiles, cosmetics, food, and drink products usually all [2] _____ food dyes. Some dyes [3] _____ from natural sources and others are synthetic. However, doctors [4] _____ that the number of people with allergic reactions to dyes [5] _____ . We [6] _____ that in a number of people some natural dyes [7] _____ rashes or respiratory problems. However, we [8] _____ why this reaction [9] _____ more common.

Grammar stative verbs

4 Read the comments by shoppers in a shopping center. Complete the comments with the simple present and present continuous form of the verbs.

1 _____ you _____ (like) this color? _____ it _____ (look) natural?

2 I _____ (look) for a shirt like this, but in a different size.

3 Excuse me. _____ this bag _____ (belong) to you?

4 What _____ it _____ (taste) like?

5 _____ you _____ (think) about buying this? It's very expensive.

6 I _____ (suppose) it's time to go home.

Vocabulary time expressions

5 Write sentences about Jamie. Use the simple present or present continuous and put the time expression in the correct position.

1 go out with friends / on weekends
_____

2 spend time with his family / today
_____

3 make lunch / at the moment
_____

1b What color is Tuesday?

Reading synesthesia

1 Read about Mark.

What color is Tuesday?

My name is Mark. I'm Canadian and I have synesthesia. It's not a disease (although I think it sounds like one) and it doesn't really have any serious effects on my day-to-day life, but it is a strange condition. Synesthesia happens when two or more of your senses get mixed up. So in my case, for example, I taste words. My sense of taste works even when I'm not eating anything, but when I hear or read certain words. For me, the word "box" tastes of eggs. That's just one example, of course.

My sister is synesthetic too and she sees words in color. So when she sees the word "Tuesday" or just thinks of the word "Tuesday," she gets the feeling of "brown." Actually that kind of synesthesia, where the days of the week are colored, is the most common type. I read somewhere that synesthesia is connected to the way our brains develop language and that there's a link between sounds and shapes. I don't understand the idea very well, but it sounds fascinating.

2 Answer the questions.

1 Is synesthesia an illness?

2 What happens when people have synesthesia?

3 Does it affect Mark's life at all?

4 How does synesthesia affect Mark's sister?

5 What's the most frequent example of synesthesia?

6 Which part of the body is involved in synesthesia?

Grammar questions

3 Write the missing word in each question. Then write the answers.

1 Where Mark come from?

2 else in his family has the same condition?

3 What the name of his condition?

4 sense gives Mark problems?

5 What color Mark's sister associate with *Tuesday*?

4 Read the statements. Use these words to write follow-up questions. You can write more than one question for each statement.

Can you … ?	What are … ?
Do you … ?	Where are … ?
How many … ?	Why do … ?

1 This is a photo of one of my brothers.

2 I work in marketing.

3 We go to France every year.

4 I like to go home for the holidays.

5 I want to learn Japanese after English.

6 I love detective stories. I read for at least three hours every day!

1c A sense of color

Reading color blindness

1 You are going to read an article about Holly, who is color-blind. First, choose the option you think is correct. Then read the article and check.

   1 Most color-blind people can't tell the difference between red and *blue / green*.
   2 Color blindness is more common in *men / women*.
   3 Our eyes have *two / three* types of cells that see color.
   4 Most color-blind people *lead / can't lead* a normal life.

2 Read the article about Holly.

I have red-green color blindness, which is the most common kind. It's something I was born with. Color blindness is quite common—about ten percent of men have some kind of color blindness. On the other hand, it's rare in women—so I'm unusual, I guess. If you have red-green color blindness, like me, it basically means that you can't tell the difference between shades of red and shades of green. They look more or less the same to me. So, for example, I can't tell if the DVD player is on or off. But they are starting to make electrical items with blue indicator lights for "on"—which is much better for people like me.

Color blindess is a problem with the cells in my eyes. Our eyes normally see color using three different kinds of cells. So one kind of cell sees red, another kind sees green, and the third kind sees blue. But if you don't have enough of one kind of cell, then this leads to color blindness. There isn't a cure for color blindness. An eye doctor can give you colored glasses or contact lenses, but they aren't very much help—at least not for me.

Finally, I think that most of the time color-blind people can lead a normal life, as long as you don't want to be a police officer or an airline pilot—there are a few jobs you just can't do.

3 Answer the questions.

   1 What percentage of men have color blindness?

   2 What problem does Holly have with her DVD player?

   3 What color is better for indicators on electrical items?

   4 What are the three colors the cells in our eyes can see?

   5 What kind of jobs are not open to color-blind people?

Word focus *see*

4 Look at two different meanings of the verb *see* from the interview. Then match the sentences with *see* (1–7) with the uses (a–g).

One kind of cell sees red. = the sense of sight

Yes, of course, I see. = showing understanding

   1 I see better with my glasses.
   2 Can you sit down? I can't see the screen.
   3 As I see it, that's the best idea.
   4 Do you see what I mean?
   5 "You have to turn it on here." "Oh, I see."
   6 I see that Janet is leaving the company.
   7 Come and see us this weekend.

   a checking understanding
   b giving news
   c giving your opinion
   d showing understanding
   e the sense of sight
   f visibility of something
   g visit someone

5 Replace four expressions in these exchanges with the correct form of *see*.
   1 A: I don't think I can help you.
      B: I understand. Well, thanks anyway.

   2 A: I'm getting a lot of headaches.
      B: You need to go to a doctor.

   3 A: Do you understand how easy it is?
      B: Oh yes. Thanks.

1d First impressions

Real life **opening and closing conversations**

1 Put the words in order to make statements and questions. Then write O for ways of opening conversations and C for ways of closing conversations.

1 a / you / pleasure / to / it's / meet

....

2 don't / card / give / why / my / I / you

.... ?

3 myself / may / introduce / I

.... ?

4 stay / touch / in / let's

....

5 you / to / talking / good / been / it's

....

6 you / to / very / I'm / meet / pleased

....

2 Complete this conversation with four of the sentences from Exercise 1.

W: Good morning! [1] .... I'm Will Marr.

G: How do you do? My name's Grace Larsen.

W: [2] ...., Grace. Are you a colleague of Daniel's?

G: Yes, I am, actually. We're both working on this project. […]

W: Well, Grace, [3] .... I'm very interested in your ideas.

G: Thanks. [4] .... You can reach me on both those numbers.

W: OK, thanks.

3 Complete these ways of talking about what you do with prepositions.

1 I work .... a design company.

2 I mostly work .... special projects.

3 I'm an administrator .... Liberty Bank.

4 I'm .... customer service.

5 I'm looking .... a new job at the moment.

6 I'm a student .... Williams College.

4 Pronunciation **short questions**

Match the comments (1–6) with the questions (a–f) to make short exchanges.

1	I'm a colleague of Daniel's.	a	Can you?
2	She is one of our best customers.	b	Do you?
3	I work in our main office.	c	Have you?
4	We've got a branch in your area.	d	Is she?
5	It's one of our biggest stores.	e	Are you?
6	I can call you tomorrow.	f	Oh, is it?

5 Grammar extra **auxiliary verbs in short questions and answers**

▶ **AUXILIARY VERBS IN SHORT QUESTIONS AND ANSWERS**

We use auxiliary verbs to make short questions and short answers. The auxiliary verbs are *be, have, do,* and modal verbs. (*Be, have,* and *do* can also be main verbs.)

Auxiliary verbs	Examples
be (am, are, is) *have (have, has)* modal verb (*can, must,* etc.) simple present (*do, does*) present continuous (*am, is, are*)	*Are you? Yes, I am.* *Has it? No, it hasn't.* *Can she? No, she can't.* *Do you? Yes, I do.* *Are they? Yes, they are.*

Write short questions or short answers in response to these comments.

1 I'm learning Greek at the moment.

....

2 This paint is selling very well.

....

3 Do you have my telephone number?
Yes, ...

4 Do you think you can win?
Yes, ...

5 Can you see what's happening?
No, ...

6 My colleagues are excited about this.

....

1e About us

Writing a profile

1 Writing skill criteria for writing: text type, style, reader, purpose, and structure

a Read the excerpts from company communications. Choose the correct option.

1 text type: *letter / website*

> I'm pleased to inform you that we are offering a new range of services.

2 style: *formal / informal*

> ## Check out our new range!
> ## We think it's really cool!

3 reader: *known / not known*

> Please note the following changes to your account.

4 purpose: *to give information / to advertise a product*

> Our clients are national and international companies.

b Read the information from a company profile. Match the sentences (a–d) with the headings (1–3). There are two sentences with one of the headings. Then use numbers with the headings to organize the information in a logical way.

Intersect Design

1 About our work | 2 Satisfied customers | 3 About us

ⓐ "We always get fantastic results when we use Intersect." *Blacks International*

ⓑ As well as this, we are working with a cell phone operator on a new campaign. We work in all areas of advertising.

ⓒ Currently, we are developing a new logo for a national radio station.

ⓓ We are a design agency with twenty years' experience.

2 Rewrite the sentences using the words in parentheses in the correct position. There is sometimes more than one possibility.

1 I am working on a new product. (this year)

2 I can help you with new projects. (also)

3 We are advising a national company. (currently)

4 We are completing a major contract. (at this time)

5 We have offices in all major cities. (in addition to this)

6 We work in TV. (too)

3 Checking accuracy

Find and correct ten spelling mistakes in this profile.

1
2
3
4
5
6
7
8
9
10

> I am a freelance designar in the fashion industry. I also work as a consultant to a sportswear manufacturer. My especial areas of interest include working with natural textiles and dies. I am currently developping a range of baby clothes which are non-alergic.
>
> Outside of work, I have a pasion for abstract art, especially the collorful works of Kandinsky. I am continualy trying to improve my own skills as a paintor.

Wordbuilding noun and verb → noun

> ▶ **WORDBUILDING noun and verb → noun**
>
> We can change the ending of some nouns and verbs to make words that describe what people do.
> *anthropology → anthropologist*
> *win → winner*

1 Complete the words in the table.

Noun/Verb	Suffix	Noun
anthropology art biology science	*-ist*	*anthropologist*
win administrate compete	*-er/-or*	*winner*
contest assist consult participate	*-ant*	*contestant*
optics electricity library music politics	*-ian*	*optician*

2 These verbs all take the same suffix. Which one?

design	learn	manage	photograph
research	speak	teach	train

3 Complete the sentences with nouns (singular or plural) from Exercises 1 and 2.

1 A .... helps you find books to borrow.

2 David Hockney is one of my favorite ....

3 Survey for seminar .... : Please give us your opinion!

4 My new glasses are ready for me at the .... 's.

5 This is a great black and white image by a local ....

6 My friend's an .... He can fix your lights for you.

Learning skills study routines

> Learning English is easier and you are more successful when you follow a routine.

4 Draw a table showing your waking hours for each day of the week. Write your activities under the times. Then choose two colors and block off times:
- when you are free to study
- when you can study at the same time as you do something else, e.g., read on the train

	7 a.m.	8 a.m.	9 a.m.	10 a.m.	11 a.m.
Monday	coffee	train	work		break

5 How long do these activities need? Write 5, 30, or 60 (minutes) next to each one.
- reviewing vocabulary
- listening
- reading a magazine or graded reader
- doing Workbook exercises
- doing interactive (CD-ROM/online) exercises
- watching a DVD
- doing homework for class

6 Match activities from Exercise 5 with color-blocked times in your table from Exercise 4.

7 Use your table to work out a realistic study routine.

Check!

8 Fill in the spaces (1–6) with places from Student Book Unit 1 and find another place.

1 Orange means "happiness" in this country.
2 There's a traditional prayer for peace here.
3 Van Gogh painted "Yellow House" here.
4 The city that Hertz rental cars and the first yellow cabs come from.
5 Blue can be a sad color in this country.
6 One of the South American countries where the Quechua people live.

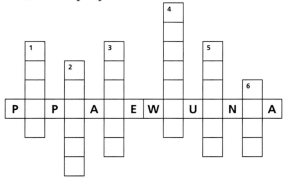

Unit 2 Performance

2a Performances

Grammar present perfect

1 Complete the sentences with the present perfect form of the verbs and *for* or *since* where necessary.

1 We _____ (be) here _____ a few weeks and we love everything we _____ (see) so far.

2 I _____ (perform) every night _____ I got here and the crowds are great.

3 We _____ (never / have) so much success before.

4 My friend _____ (live) here _____ a couple of months and now I _____ (decide) to join her.

5 I _____ (always / want) to sing in public and now I can. _____ I came here, I _____ (become) more confident.

6 I _____ (not / hear) this music before. It's quite unusual.

2 Rewrite the sentences adding *already*, *just*, or *yet*.

1 Have you seen *Billy Elliot*?

2 Don't get me a ticket. I've bought mine.

3 I can't meet you later. I haven't finished my work.

4 We've been to see Lady Gaga. Wow!

5 I arrived this morning and I've seen dozens of performances.

6 I'm not sure what that means! I've started learning Spanish.

Vocabulary musical styles

3 Write one of these words for each sentence.

catchy	cheerful	lively	melancholy
melodic	moving	repetitive	rhythmic
tuneless	unusual		

1 This music has an interesting and pleasant tune.

2 It's different from anything you've ever heard before.

3 It's good for dancing to.

4 You can't stop singing it once you've heard it.

5 It's a little bit sad.

6 It's not really pleasant to listen to.

7 Every song sounds the same to me.

4 Writing street performers

In many cities street performers are in parks, public squares, and train stations. Describe the street performers you have seen.

2b One of a kind

Grammar verb patterns: -ing form and to + infinitive

1 Complete the sentences with these words.

I agreed	I keep	My schedule
I finished	I need	We decided
I hope	I really enjoy	

1 _____ teaching my students to sing.
2 _____ to teach music when I graduate from college.
3 _____ making mistakes when I dance.
4 _____ to make more progress with my performance.
5 _____ involves getting up early every day.
6 _____ to involve the audience in our performance.
7 _____ taking classes last year.
8 _____ to take a role in the play.

2 Match the questions (a–b) with the sentences (1–9). Then complete the questions and sentences with the correct form of the verbs in parentheses.

a I'm thinking about _____ (go) to the circus next week. Do you want _____ (come)?

b What have you decided _____ (do) for your birthday?

1 I intend _____ (take) it easy this year.
2 I think it's too late _____ (get) tickets.
3 I'm hoping _____ (go) to the theater.
4 I'm not sure. I keep _____ (change) my mind.
5 No, thanks. I don't enjoy _____ (watch) animals perform.
6 Nothing special. I'm no good at _____ (plan).
7 Nothing yet. But my friends have promised _____ (not / give) me a surprise party.

8 OK, why not? I need _____ (do) something different.
9 _____ (see) animals doing tricks isn't my idea of entertainment.

3 Grammar extra *remember*, *stop*, and *try*

> ▶ REMEMBER, STOP, and TRY
>
> Both the *-ing* form and *to* + infinitive can follow these verbs, but there is a change in meaning.
>
> *stop* + *-ing* refers to the **activity** which stops:
> *I only **stop practicing** when the studio closes.*
>
> *stop* + *to* + infinitive *refers to the **reason** for stopping:*
> *I usually **stop to rest** when I'm tired.*

Complete the sentences with the *-ing* form and *to* + infinitive form of the verbs.

1 When I'm tired, I stop _____ (dance).
2 If a new student comes in, we stop _____ (introduce) ourselves.
3 I usually remember _____ (change) my clothes before I paint.
4 I'm trying _____ (find) a way of keeping in touch with old friends.
5 I've tried _____ (join) Facebook, but most of my friends don't use it.

4 Complete the sentences with these words.

cheer up	cry	cry	laugh	laughing
sad	smile	smile	smile	

1 Don't _____ . It's only a movie.
2 Come on! _____ for the camera!
3 _____ ! It's not the end of the world.
4 The situation was so absurd we didn't know whether to _____ or _____ .
5 It's great to hear you _____ for a change. You've seemed _____ recently.
6 Have you noticed? When you _____ at people, they _____ back.

2c Life in a day

Reading a movie review

Read a review of the movie *Life in a Day*.

The experimental film *Life in a Day* is quite unusual. It gives us a picture of life in our world—the whole world—on one single day: July 24, 2010. The movie is a documentary—not a drama or a thriller or a romantic comedy. But at the same time, it has moments of drama and of romance. In fact, the movie is simply a lot of moments—90 minutes of moments from people's lives around the world on that July 24. Some of these moments are connected, some aren't. Sometimes during these 90 minutes, it's difficult to concentrate. Watching it becomes almost exhausting. So many images flash in front of your eyes. But the idea of the movie is certainly interesting. The movie itself is made from videos shot by ordinary people. There are no actors or professional film-makers or special effects. And although there is no story, there are themes: love, fear, hope, and so on.

The project began when director Kevin Macdonald had an idea: "to take the temperature of the planet on a single day," as he puts it. He sent about 400 cameras to 40 countries and asked people three questions: "What do you love? What do you fear? What have you got in your pocket?" Then people used the cameras to film their lives, or the lives of those around them, and sent the footage back to Macdonald. And the astonishing thing was that the project grew to be much bigger than 400 people with cameras. A week after the "day," Macdonald and his team had 4,500 hours of footage in 81,000 video clips from 192 countries. Even more astonishing, perhaps, was the fact that at that stage, Macdonald didn't have a plan for his movie. He wanted to see all the footage first and try to choose 90 minutes from that.

So, what did he choose? What kind of movie do we get? There are women in Ghana singing while they work, an English student talking with his dad, men in India gossiping, market sellers in the Philippines having lunch…the list goes on. And there are words to go with the images too. The faces speak to us, telling us that they "love football" or "are afraid of growing up." The movie has been pretty successful—perhaps more than Macdonald expected. If you've missed it in the theater, you can watch it on YouTube. It's an interesting way to spend an hour and a half.

1 What is the reviewer's opinion of the movie? Choose one option (a–c).

- a   It's an unusual idea, but in the end it's a boring movie.
- b   It's one of the best movies she's ever seen.
- c   It's an interesting idea that has mainly succeeded.

Word focus *have*

2 Match the excerpts (1–8) from the movie review with the uses of *have* (a–e).

1   It has moments of drama.
2   Kevin Macdonald had an idea.
3   What do you have in your pocket?
4   Macdonald and his team had 4,500 hours of footage.
5   Macdonald didn't have a plan.
6   market sellers in the Philippines having lunch…
7   The movie has been pretty successful.
8   If you've missed it…

- a   an auxiliary verb (with the present perfect)
- b   an auxiliary verb (with *do*)
- c   a main verb (ownership or possession)
- d   a main verb (past tense, without *do*)
- e   a main verb (collocation with a noun)

3 Complete the sentences with the correct form of *have*.

1   We _____ a great time last night.
2   Kevin Macdonald _____ made some great movies.
3   _____ you _____ any of his movies on DVD?
4   Let's _____ dessert after the show.
5   I _____ never been to Los Angeles.
6   Do you want to _____ lunch early today?
7   They're _____ a party after the movie preview.
8   They _____ some problems with the cameras at first.

2d What's on?

Real life **choosing an event**

1 Complete each suggestion in two ways.

1 ....
.... see a movie tonight?

2 ....
.... seeing a movie tonight?

2 Respond to this suggestion in three ways.

"Let's go to the MegaScreen—the new Russell Crowe movie is on."

....

....

....

3 Write questions for these answers.

1 ....
There's a jazz concert at City Hall Plaza.

2 ....
I think it's by Abi Morgan.

3 ....
It has that guy who was in *Lost*.

4 ....
There's a late show at 11 p.m.

5 ....
It's the story of a young boy who loves dancing.

Vocabulary **describing performances**

4 Rewrite the sentences about performances as comments using these words. You can use the words in bold more than once.

| **absolutely** | awful | boring | outstanding |
| disappointing | good | hilarious | **really** **very** |

1 It was the funniest comedy show you've ever been to.
It was absolutely hilarious.

2 It was the worst concert you've ever been to.
....

3 You fell asleep during the play.
....

4 The exhibition was better than average.
....

5 You expected the performance to be better.
....

6 It was the best movie you've ever seen.
....

Grammar extra **adjectives ending in -*ed* and -*ing***

> ▶ **ADJECTIVES ENDING IN -*ED* and -*ING***
>
> We use the present participle and past participle of some verbs as adjectives: *bore → bored → boring*
>
> -*ed* adjectives describe a person's state: *I'm bored. I was amazed.*
>
> -*ing* adjectives describe the characteristics of a thing or person: *It was boring. They were amazing.*

5 Complete the sentences with the -*ed* or -*ing* form of these verbs.

| amaze | bore | depress | disappoint | fascinate |
| move | | | | |

1 With so many choices, how can you say you're
.... ?

2 Those acrobats were ....
I don't know how they do that.

3 To be honest, I felt .... by the lack of originality.

4 It's impossible not to be .... by such beautiful music.

5 Another movie about terrible childhoods? How
.... !

6 What a .... play that was! I'm still thinking about it now.

2e A portrait of an artist

Writing skill linking ideas

1 Read the sentences about the Indian musician Ravi Shankar. Cross out any options that are incorrect.

1 He started working with the Beatles in 1966, *so / therefore* he was instantly in the spotlight.

2 *Although / While* he's young in his mind, his body is too frail to play an instrument.

3 *Despite / In spite of* his age, he still enjoys music by artists such as Lady Gaga.

4 English music is written down. *In contrast, / For that reason,* Indian music is often improvised.

5 He appreciates most art forms, *but / so* he doesn't like electronic music.

2 Rewrite the sentences with the words in parentheses. Make any changes to verbs and punctuation as necessary.

a Even though he's from a classical Indian background, he's had mainstream success in the West. (despite)

b He played on Beatles records, so he quickly became well-known in Europe. (because of this)

c In spite of enjoying the music he made with the Beatles, he didn't like the attention it brought. (although)

d He loves Matisse and Picasso. Nevertheless, he doesn't believe in owning art. (while)

e He began as a dancer. However, he became more interested in making music. (but)

f In spite of not knowing much about classical Indian music, I love his work. (although)

3 Complete the sentences with the correct form of the verbs in parentheses. Then decide which sentences (a–f) from Exercise 2 go in the boxes. Write the complete profile in your notebook.

1 Ravi Shankar is a classical Indian musician who _____ (have) huge success over many decades.

2 I _____ (follow) his work since I _____ (see) him on TV a few years ago. ☐

3 This _____ (begin) decades ago when he _____ (work) with George Harrison, of the Beatles. ☐

4 Of course, I'm too young _____ (remember) the Beatles.

5 I enjoy the music he _____ (make) nowadays. ☐

6 I like it because it _____ (sound) beautiful and unusual to me. It's really different from Western music.

7 There's so much different stuff out there _____ (listen) to, and I enjoy it all.

Wordbuilding **adjective + noun**

> ▶ **WORDBUILDING adjective + noun**
>
> Some adjectives and nouns often go together.
> *outside world*   *popular culture*

1 Match the adjectives with the nouns. They are all in the Student Book or Workbook Unit 2. More than one combination is possible.

> **Adjectives**
> bad big English famous living mainstream
> ordinary romantic special traditional young

> **Nouns**
> actor comedies couple effects influence
> mood people role statue student success

2 Complete the sentences with adjective + noun combinations from Exercise 1.

1 The Beatles were a _____ on many pop groups.
2 The _____ in the apartment next door are really friendly.
3 This band has been around for a couple of years but hasn't had _____ yet.
4 The actress Meg Ryan appeared in a lot of _____ early in her career.
5 My favorite movies have amazing

_____ that l can believe in.
6 If I'm in a _____, listening to music helps me feel more cheerful.

Learning skills **mistakes**

> Making mistakes is part of learning. Thinking about mistakes in different categories can help you.

3 Look at these types of mistakes. Try to write down an example of each kind of mistake.

- mistakes you make because you haven't learned the correct word or structure yet

- mistakes that are common to all learners with the same first language as you

- mistakes that you make when speaking because you don't have enough time to think about what you say

- mistakes that are "yours"—things you personally have problems with

- mistakes that mean people can't understand your message properly

4 Do you make mistakes with any of these things? Write an example.

1 the verb tense in sentences like *I haven't met many people since I moved here.*

2 the verb form in constructions like *Listening to music helps me feel more cheerful.*

3 adjectives like *bored/boring*

5 Keep a record of mistakes you make often. Think about what kind of mistake they are. Write down the correct language and try to remember it. But don't worry too much about the mistakes that don't affect how well people understand you. And don't worry if it takes a while to correct your mistakes.

Check!

6 Read these descriptions. The first letter of each word described below spells a word. What it is it?

1 A photo or painting of a person.	1	
2 Actors, comedians, acrobats, singers, etc. are all… .	2	
3 Music from Jamaica.	3	
4 A style of music and dance from southern Spain.	4	
5 A large group of people who play musical instruments together.	5	
6 The title of one of Baz Luhrmann's movies.	6	
7 Someone who does clever tricks for an audience.	7	
8 Really, really bad.	8	
9 Joining a club is a good way of making…friends.	9	
10 A group of people who sing together.	10	
11 A kind of coffee.	11	

Unit 3 Water

3a Underwater

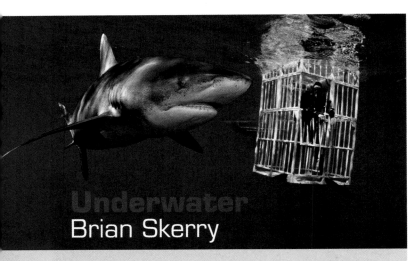

Underwater
Brian Skerry

1 Finding the oceanic whitetip shark is an experience I won't forget. This is one of the most dangerous sharks in the world, but its numbers are falling. They used to be common around the Bahamas, but most people say they haven't seen them for years. Just as we arrived there, some sports fishermen in the central Bahamas saw some oceanic whitetips when they were fishing for tuna. So I planned sixteen days to go searching for them.

For the first few days out of Palm Beach, we didn't see a thing. Then, on the fifth day, I was looking out from the bridge when I spotted a shark on the surface. The white tip of its dorsal fin was sticking out of the water, so I knew we had an oceanic whitetip. I quickly put on my wetsuit and jumped in the water. The shark was very curious about me and swam right up to me. It was about ten feet long and it even stayed around while we were putting the cage in the water for the scientist. I got some great pictures! That was really the high point of the assignment.

2 At the end of the assignment, after a year of work, we were going after the great hammerhead shark. This species is so elusive that there were no pictures of it up until five or six years ago. For the entire first week, the weather was appalling and it was impossible to dive. It was very frustrating. Then, on the eighth day, my assistant had to fly home because his mother was seriously ill.

Suddenly, I was working alone as well as trying to deal with the bad weather. That was definitely the worst moment on the assignment. It is so important to have a really good assistant with you. Without him there, my workload more than doubled. While I was trying to decide what to do, the weather unexpectedly improved and I got a couple of not-bad days! And on one of those days, everything clicked and I got some great pictures of a hammerhead. I was lucky.

Reading **on assignment**

1 Find these words and expressions in the text. Choose the correct option.

1 spotted: *photographed / saw*
2 high point: *best moment / top of the boat*
3 deal with: *survive / solve the problem*
4 workload: *amount of work you have to do / problems*
5 doubled: *increased by twice as much / increased by three times as much*
6 clicked: *was quiet / was successful*

Grammar **simple past and past continuous**

2 Write questions for these answers. Use the information from the article.

1 When _____ ?
   When they were fishing for tuna.
2 When _____ ?
   While he was looking out from the bridge.
3 How _____ ?
   Because the white tip of its dorsal fin was sticking out of the water.
4 What _____ ?
   They were going after the great hammerhead shark.
5 What _____ ?
   Skerry's assistant flew home.
6 What _____ ?
   He was trying to decide what to do.

3b Problems and rescues

Reading Hurricane Mitch

1 You are going to read the introduction to an article about hurricanes. Check (✓) the words you think you will find. Then read and check.

clouds	destructive	flooded	ocean
powerful	rainfall	sand	tornado
tropical	waves	wet	winds

Hurricanes are giant, wet, and windy tropical storms. They bring strong winds and heavy rainfall. Hurricanes begin in the Atlantic Ocean and there is an annual season from mid-August to late October.

One of the wettest and most destructive hurricanes in recent history was Hurricane Mitch. It hit the Caribbean and Central America in November 1998. By the time Mitch reached the coast, most people had already left the area. When the danger had passed and people had returned home, they couldn't believe what had happened. In Honduras, farmland had turned into desert. Bridges and roads had disappeared. Rivers had changed course. As Mitch passed over Honduras, so much rain fell that some rivers flooded to six times their normal size. In one day, the area had the equivalent of 200 days of rainfall. In places where there had been rivers with lines of trees, now there was nothing. The trees had all washed away. This kind of thing is not so unusual during hurricanes, but the power of Mitch was extreme. The tremendous winds had picked up sand and carried it for many miles before dropping it in a new area. Suddenly, there was a desert where people had had farms. Mitch had completely changed the land and, of course, the lives of the people who lived there. It took them many years to recover. And although there will be hurricanes in the future as powerful as Mitch, the World Meteorological Organization decided the name Mitch will never be used again.

2 Choose the correct option (a–c).

1 Hurricanes begin in the .... Ocean.
  a Atlantic   b Indian   c Pacific

2 There is a hurricane season every ....
  a month   b year   c ten years

3 Hurricane Mitch affected .... America.
  a North and South b the Caribbean and South
  c the Caribbean and Central

4 .... rain fell in one day in Honduras.
  a Six days'   b Two months'
  c Two hundred days'

3 What happened to these things during Hurricane Mitch? What was responsible: wind or water?

1 bridges

2 farmland

3 rivers

4 roads

5 sand

6 trees

Grammar past perfect

4 Change the verbs to the past perfect where necessary.

1 By the time the storm reached land, most residents left the area. ....

2 When people got back home, they were amazed at what happened. ....

3 In some places, before the hurricane there were trees, but now there was nothing.
....

4 Many roads and bridges disappeared by the end of the first day. ....

5 After the hurricane, there was a desert where people had farms. ....

6 It became clear how much changed when people saw the satellite images. ....

3c Bottled water

Reading water on tap?

Read the article about Bundanoon, a bottled water free town in Australia.

Bundanoon is a small town near Sydney, Australia. It has its own supply of water from an underground water reserve. Some years ago, the residents of the town discovered that a water company had applied for permission to extract this water, bottle it, and sell it as drinking water. Bundanoon resident Pauline Tiller explains why she and other people in town didn't want this water company to go ahead with their plans.

"We were drinking the water in our homes, direct from our taps. We didn't want to buy bottled water—especially when it was already our own town's water supply! Then one morning something in the newspaper caught my attention. It was an astonishing letter Huw Kingston had written about banning bottled water.

"Huw is a local businessman, and he had come up with this revolutionary idea—he wanted the town to fight the water company. And he also wanted us to ban bottled water completely! As soon as I read his letter, I knew that was the answer!

"So a few residents got together to investigate how we could go 'bottled water free.' Then we found out that the carbon footprint of bottled water is 300 times greater than tap water! It became obvious that bottled water is a crazy idea. So we had a town meeting to discuss the whole thing and the town decided to become 'bottled water free.' After that a lot of national and international newspapers had heard about our story. After they wrote about us, we got a lot of support from environmental movements. And in September 2009, we became the first 'bottled water free' town in Australia.

"Now all the water in our town is free, so you can get it from the tap. And if you want to take some water with you, our shops sell our own 'Bundanoon' reusable bottles. Vistors can buy one and fill it up."

1 Answer the questions.

1 Where does Bundanoon get its water from?

2 What did the water company want to do?

3 What had local businessman Huw Kingston done?

4 What happened at the town meeting?

5 When did environmental groups start to support the town?

Word focus *get*

2 Look at these sentences from the story about Bundanoon. Replace the words in bold with four of these words. There is one extra word.

become	entered	met	obtain	received

1 And how did you **get** involved in the story?

2 A few residents **got together** to investigate how we could go "bottled water free."

3 After they wrote about us, we **got** a lot of support from environmental movements.

4 All the water in our town is free, so you can **get** it from the tap.

3 Match the comments (1–6) with the responses (a–f).

1 How did it go at the meeting?

2 This company wants to bottle the town's water.

3 Can you get me a paper when you go to the store?

4 How's the campaign going?

5 How did you get your picture in the papers?

6 What a crazy week!

a We just got in touch with the reporters about the campaign.

b I don't get it. Why do they want to do that?

c I know! I can't wait for things to get back to normal.

d Very well. Our suggestions got a lot of support.

e Things are getting better now that we've been on TV.

f Yes, sure.

3d No way!

Real life telling stories

1 Complete the story with these words.

after	during	later	suddenly	then	while

Did I ever tell you about the time I went fishing with my best friend's father? ¹ _____ the drive to the lake, he told me about all the huge fish he'd caught. ² _____ half an hour of this, I wanted to go home. Anyway, we'd been on the lake for a couple of hours when ³ _____ , my fishing rod started to move. ⁴ _____ I was trying to bring the fish in, he was shouting, "It's huge, really big!" Thirty minutes ⁵ _____ , I still hadn't managed to get the fish in the boat. And ⁶ _____ I dropped my rod in the water. My best friend's father was horrified. He never spoke to me again.

2 Grammar extra *when/while/as*

> ▶ *WHEN/WHILE/AS*
>
> We can use *when*, *while*, and *as* to show that two actions happened *at the same time*.
>
> Use *when* with a short action (past simple) which happened during a longer action:
> *We were sitting in the boat when my fishing rod moved.*
>
> Use *while* for two longer actions:
> *While I was trying to control it, he was shouting.*
>
> Use *as* for two short actions:
> *As I stepped forward, I dropped the rod.*

Circle the best option.

1 We were driving to the river *while / when* we ran out of gas.
2 *As / While* I got out of the car, I felt the rain.
3 *While / When* we were putting gas in the car, the sky was getting darker.
4 *As / When* I walked to the cash register, I decided to go home.
5 We were talking about our plans *while / when* my phone rang.
6 *As / While* I got back home, the sun came out.

Grammar review simple past and past continuous

3 Complete the sentences with the simple past or past continuous form of the verbs in parentheses.

1 We _____ a shark when we _____ . (see / surf)
2 I _____ back into the boat when I _____ my camera into the water. (climb / drop)
3 It _____ a beautiful morning. The sun _____ over the horizon and the fish _____ . (be / come up / jump)
4 It _____ to rain while we _____ a really good sequence. (start / movie)
5 We _____ in the boat, quickly _____ our equipment, and _____ home. (get / pack up / go)
6 While we _____ back to land, the wind suddenly _____ a lot stronger. (sail / get)

Vocabulary review water and recreation

4 Write these words in the correct place.

canoeing	diving	fishing	jet-skiing
kayaking	rafting	rowing	parasailing
sailing	scuba diving	snorkeling	surfing
swimming	synchronized swimming		water
polo	water-skiing	windsurfing	

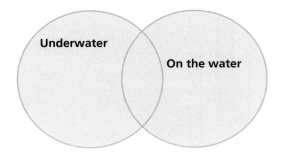

Underwater

On the water

3e What a weekend!

Writing a blog post

1 Jenna's computer has made a mess of her blog. Put the text in the correct order. Write numbers next to the lines.

Titanic Fanatics trip to Belfast

Well, that certainly was a weekend to remember! After months of	a _1_
embarking on a new life. The entire experience was	b _____
<u>here</u>.	c _____
members of the *Titanic Fanatics Society*, and we unexpectedly	d _____
especially moving as I thought about all those heroic passengers	e _____
On Saturday morning we made our way to the spectacular	f _____
completely packed, of course—nobody wanted to miss the centenary	g _____
planning, we finally made it to Belfast to see where the whole	h _____
bumped into some familiar faces on Friday evening too. The hotel was	i _____
Wandering slowly through the authentically recreated cabins was	j _____
Titanic Belfast center. It was thrilling to see the place where	k _____
Titanic was designed, built, and launched a century ago.	l _____
tragic *Titanic* story began. There were sixteen of us altogether, all	m _____
unforgettable and you can see all my photos and read more	n _____
weekend.	o _____

2 Writing skill interesting language

a Match these words with the expressions Jenna used.

> amazing   arrived in   emotional   exciting
> full of people   met   some friends   sad   starting
> went

1 we finally **made it to** Belfast: _____
2 **tragic** story: _____
3 we **bumped into** some **familiar faces**: _____
   _____
4 **packed**: _____
5 we **made our way** to: _____
6 spectacular: _____
7 thrilling: _____
8 moving: _____
9 **embarking on** a new life: _____

b Complete the sentences with words from Exercise 2a.

1 The new aquatic sports building is _____ .
2 I _____ my boss at the movie theater.
3 It was rush hour, so the bus was _____ .
4 I got on the train and _____ to my seat.
5 I was surprised to see _____ at the exhibition.
6 This young boy had a _____ life before going to the US.

3 Look at the words. Find four words to describe:

1 a view: _____ , _____ ,
   _____ ,
2 an experience: _____ , _____ ,
   _____ ,
3 a place you are in: _____ , _____ ,
   _____ ,
4 ways of "going": _____ , _____ ,
   _____ ,

impressive packed
exciting magnificent travel
crowded exhilarating **spectacular**
busy electrifying take off thrilling
full fabulous **move on**   **set off**

4 Use these notes to write the second part of Jenna's blog in your notebook.

- Saturday evening / got dressed up
- dinner / spectacular dining room
- whole thing / recreation / dinner on *Titanic*
- dining room / packed / thrilling / costumes
- bumped into / people / earlier / joined
- food / amazing / whole thing / moving

Wordbuilding adverbs

> ► **WORDBUILDING adverbs**
>
> Most adverbs are formed by adding -ly to adjectives. Some adverbs and adjectives are the same.
> *quick* (adjective) → *quickly* (adverb)
> *fast* (adjective) = *fast* (adverb)

1 Make adverbs from these adjectives. The adverbs are all in the Student Book or Workbook Units 1–3.

complete	definite	easy	extreme	fast
fortunate	normal	quick	serious	slow
unexpected	unpleasant	unsuccessful		

2 How many ways can you complete these sentences? Use adjectives or adverbs from Exercise 1.

1 The raft came down the river really… .

2 …, this doesn't happen often.

3 He's a rather…person.

4 We were…lost.

5 I made several…attempts and then gave up.

6 The hippo…turned towards us.

Learning skills keeping a journal

3 One of the most difficult things about learning English is remembering everything. Keeping a journal can help you. Look at the page from a journal and check (✓) the things the student has included.
- diagrams/drawings
- example sentences
- grammar
- how he/she feels about something
- listening
- other students
- pictures
- questions for the teacher
- reading
- reminders to do things
- self-evaluation
- speaking
- test scores
- vocabulary
- writing

Nov 3	8/10 on a vocabulary test! ☺
Nov 6	
new words	ship<u>wreck</u> iceberg nearby edge
grammar	
reading	The reading text was difficult! <u>Read it again</u> this weekend.
	Paola told me about going through the Channel tunnel – very funny.
sentence	I <u>got back</u> home at 11.30.
Nov 10	We watched a DVD about water in India.

4 Look at the things in the diary entry that are underlined. Why do you think the student has underlined them?

Check!

5 All these words go with *water*. Which ones are in the word square? Use the clues to help you.

boiling	bottled	clean	deep	dirty	fresh
hot	rain	river	running	salt	sea	tap

X	F	L	H	H	N	I	E	K	O
H	R	I	R	U	N	N	I	N	G
A	E	B	S	E	L	A	Z	B	I
R	S	O	Q	V	O	B	U	O	T
E	H	I	P	N	H	O	T	Y	S
O	A	L	Z	I	P	T	E	W	A
R	A	I	N	P	L	T	I	R	L
P	L	N	I	E	U	L	T	T	T
E	B	G	S	U	A	E	N	B	O
Y	U	V	C	O	L	D	X	R	U

1 It falls from the sky and you can collect it in a tank.
2 Some people only drink this kind, but it's expensive.
3 Lakes are almost always this kind of water.
4 When your home gets a continuous supply from pipes.
5 If you're in this kind of water, it means you have done something wrong.
6 This kind is needed to make a cup of tea.
7 The oceans of the world are made of this.

Unit 4 Opportunities

4a Future world

Grammar predictions with *will*

1 Complete the predictions with one word so that they are 100 percent certain. Sometimes more than one option is correct.

1 The world _____ be a very different place in a few years' time. I'm sure of that.
2 He _____ (not) quit school at 16 like I did.
3 Robots and computers _____ take care of all the routine, boring things.
4 She _____ won't work full-time.
5 They'll _____ find cures for many of the health problems we face today.

2 Complete the predictions with one word so that they are NOT 100 percent certain. Sometimes more than one option is correct.

1 She'll _____ live to be 100.
2 She _____ get sick at some point in her life.
3 This _____ affect their world in ways we haven't imagined.
4 They _____ not learn it at school.
5 That _____ be a challenge!

3 Read the first sentence. Then choose the logical prediction (a or b).

1 We're going to have a baby.
   a It might be a girl.
   b It will be a girl.
2 My son has a cold.
   a He may get better soon.
   b He'll get better soon.
3 People are living longer these days.
   a I could live to be 100.
   b I'll live to be 100.
4 Electric cars are on sale now.
   a Some people might buy them.
   b Some people will buy them.

Vocabulary jobs

4 Complete and rewrite the words that describe these jobs.

1 movie star: xctng and glmrs
   _____, _____
2 fire fighter: dngrs and dmdng
   _____, _____
3 train driver: rspnsbl and rtn
   _____, _____
4 vet: rwdng and stsfyng
   _____, _____

5 Complete the sentences with the correct form of *job* or *work*.

1 The project will bring lots of new _____ to the area.
2 Do you enjoy _____ here?
3 How often do you take a day off _____ ?
4 How can you do three _____ at once? That's impossible!
5 She's got a lot to do at _____ at the moment.
6 What's your _____ ?

6 Read about Maria and decide what her job is.

a an accountant
b a manager
c a technician

Maria works for a large multinational company. Her hours are from 9 a.m. to 5 p.m., Monday to Friday. She uses a computer all day and is very good at math. Her job is routine, but it's secure and well-paid. She hopes to be promoted soon.

4b Now what?

Vocabulary education

1 Complete the questions with these expressions. Then answer the questions.

drop out of college	leave school
get a degree	pass a test
get a job	retake a test
go to college	stay in school

In your country:

1   At what age can you legally _____
_____ ?

2   Do many teenagers _____
after compulsory education?

3   What is the minimum grade you need to
_____ ?

4   How many times can you _____
_____ after you fail it?

5   Do people _____ close to
home or in other towns?

6   Is it easy to _____ in a
factory?

7   How many years does it take to _____
_____ ?

8   Do many people _____ and
get a job instead?

Word focus *do*

2 Complete the sentences with these words.

do you	homework
hair and make-up	the grocery shopping
nothing	very well

1   How _____ do? I'm Mr. Erikson.
2   My sister's doing _____ in school.
3   Are you going to do your own
_____ for the wedding?

4   I'll do _____ tomorrow—it's too late
to go now.

5   Sometimes the best solution is to do
_____ .

6   I'm going to do all of my _____
tonight.

Grammar future forms

3 Look at the uses of future forms (a–c) and the example. Then write sentences using the appropriate form as in the example.

a   a plan or intention decided before the moment of speaking
b   a decision made at the moment of speaking
c   an arrangement to do something at a specified (or understood) time in the future

Example:

I / look for a new job (a)
I'm going to look for a new job.

1   I / start my new job next week (c)
_____

2   I / meet you tonight (b)
_____

3   we / move to a new house soon (c)
_____

4   my friend / drop out of college (a)
_____

5   my friend / take a test tomorrow (c)
_____

6   I / help you study (b)
_____

7   I / see you later (b)
_____

4c Looking ahead

Vocabulary pay and conditions

1 Choose the best option.

1 I'll see you at three. I can get off early because I'm on *flex-time / overtime.*

2 It's hard to feel motivated when we haven't had a *bonus / pay raise* for seven years.

3 I love working in a clothes store, especially because they give *staff discounts / pensions* on the products!

4 We sold more than we expected, so I think we'll all get a *bonus / pay raise* this month.

5 I'm working this Sunday—it's *flex-time / overtime,* so the pay is good.

6 I won't be able to come traveling with you. I only get one week of *long hours / paid vacation* this year.

Reading Internet generation

It's been more than 20 years since the birth of the Internet. Read some comments from members of the "Internet generation"—people who were born at the same time as the Internet. What's life like for this generation and how do they view what's ahead? To find out read about Anton and Carey say.

I don't believe in making plans. Plans are for old people. I like to be spontaneous. I want to enjoy myself right now. I don't want to make any long-term plans. I have a job, and work is fine, and I'll probably be promoted soon. I work hard, earn a good salary. And I like to spend it! —Anton

My main goal right now is to get a full-time job—because I'm still in the part-time job I've had since I was in school. But I'm not worried. Something will come along, for sure. I'll try anything… I believe you have to go through life with an open mind, or you might miss an opportunity. —Carey

2 Read the article. Choose the correct option (a–c).

1 How old is the Internet?
a less than fifteen years old
b between twenty and thirty years old
c more than forty years old

2 What do we call the occasion when you are given your college degree?
a final meeting
b graduation ceremony
c leaving party

3 What do we call the occasion married couples celebrate every year?
a engagement party
b marriage ceremony
c wedding anniversary

3 Are the sentences true (T) or false (F)?

1 Anton doesn't want to settle down yet.

2 Anton's job pays well.

3 Carey is about to start college.

4 Carey isn't working at the moment.

4 Answer the questions using information from the article.

1 What is the "Internet generation"?

2 What does Anton say about plans?

3 Why does Carey believe you need an open mind?

4d Would you mind…?

Vocabulary **job requirements**

1 Choose the best option.

1 Researchers need to be *creative / well-organized* because they deal with lots of information.

2 Entrepreneurs need to be *methodical / self-confident* to make their ideas succeed.

3 Farmers need to be *creative / independent* if they are self-employed.

4 Accountants need to be *energetic / methodical* because their work is very detailed.

5 Managers need to be *creative / well-organized* when trying to solve problems.

6 Technicians need to be *conscientious / self-confident* because their work can be routine.

2 Grammar extra **predictions with *going to***

> ▶ **PREDICTIONS WITH *GOING TO***
>
> We can use *going to* to make a prediction based on something that means the speaker thinks it is certain to happen:
> *My company is in trouble. I'm going to lose my job.*

Match the situations (1–4) with the predictions (a–d).

1 I'm so nervous about this interview.

2 The interview was awful.

3 The other candidate was more experienced.

4 Your resume is really strong.

a They aren't going to offer me the job.

b She's going to get the job.

c You're going to get an interview.

d It's going to be a disaster.

Real life **making and responding to requests**

3 Use combinations of these words to complete the requests. You can use the words more than once.

all right	be	can	could	do	if	is
it	mind	OK	to	will	would	you

1 _____ reading this letter for me?

2 _____ I used your computer?

3 _____ have a look at this application form?

4 _____ give your name?

5 _____ be able to help me tomorrow?

6 _____ I borrow your phone?

4e I enclose my resume

Writing skill formal style

1 Which of these things (a–d) is not a feature of formal letters?

   a   concise sentences
   b   formal phrases to begin sentences
   c   contractions
   d   standard phrases to open and close the letter

2 Rewrite the phrases and sentences in the appropriate style for a cover letter.

   1   Hi Mr. Brown,

   2   I saw your ad.

   3   Here's my application form.

   4   I'm a fun kind of person.

   5   I've done this kind of work before.

   6   Do you want to interview me soon?

   7   Send me an email or text me.

   8   Take care,

3 Read the profile and the ad. Underline the sections in the ad that correspond to the profile information.

Profile: Manuel Santos

- enthusiastic
- hard-working
- enjoys working with people

Wants: a job in catering

Experience: restaurants, cafeterias (US, Brazil)

Availability: now

AROMA CAFÉS

   Home   About   Jobs

We are an expanding chain of specialty cafés looking for outgoing, energetic waiters/waitresses.

- part-time position leading to full-time opportunity

You will be responsible for

- serving customers
- maintaining stock
- maintaining a clean environment

Characteristics of ideal candidates are:

- some experience in catering or retail
- excellent communication skills
- hard-working and good under pressure
- authorized to work in the US

Send application form and cover letter to:
Jim.Kapoor@aroma
Ref 119/XG Closing date October 31

4 Write a cover email from Manual Santos to go with the completed application form for this job.

Wordbuilding phrasal verbs

> **WORDBUILDING phrasal verbs**
>
> We often use phrasal verbs when talking about our actions.
> *drop out*
> *get off*

1 Match the two parts of the sentences.

1 My son's just failed another test. I hope he doesn't *drop out*
2 My daughter *comes back*
3 Do you *get off*
4 I didn't finish the last question on the test—I *ran out*
5 No interesting job offers have *turned up*,
6 I'm only 23, so I don't plan to *settle down*
7 Everyone in this store *punches in*

a at 8 a.m., even the manager!
b at school, but I need to earn some money.
c for many years.
d from college every weekend with her laundry!
e of time!
f of college.
g work earlier on Fridays?

2 Complete these sentences with some of the phrasal verbs from Exercise 1.

1 Could I borrow a pen? Mine has .... of ink.
2 I hate my new job! Can I .... and work for you again?
3 We had an interview arranged, but the candidate didn't ....
4 Don't .... just because things are getting difficult.
5 Can you .... work this afternoon? I need your help at home.
6 Young people seem to .... much later nowadays.

Learning skills recording new words (1)

3 Look at the strategies (a–e). Write notes for these words. Which information helps you remember how to use the word? Which do you usually record in your notebook?

hard-working: ....

full-time: ....

enclose: ....

a how to say it in your own language
b how to pronounce it
c what kind of word it is (noun, adjective, verb, adverb)
d how to use it (example sentences)
e when to use it (in writing or speaking)

4 Organizing new words into groups can help you remember them. How many words from Unit 4 can you add to each group?

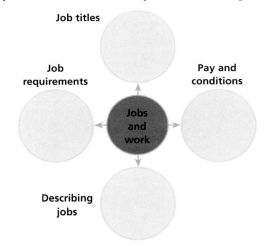

Check!

5 Answer these questions. Then use the first letters of five of the answers to give the name of a country from Unit 4.

1 If you don't like your current job, look for a .... one.
2 Something every child has when they think about their future: ....
3 Another word for a plan you have made: something you .... to do.
4 A place where workers mass-produce things: ....
5 A place you can go to earn a degree: ....
6 All employers want their employees to be this: ....

	1	2	3	4	5	6
Letters						
Word						

Unit 5 Travel

5a Business or pleasure?

Reading a travel journalist

Business or pleasure?

By Keith Bellows

Boyd Matson is one of the great travel journalists of our day. I've been a big fan of his work for years and I've "traveled" to many places through his reports, radio shows, and news columns. No stranger to adventure, Matson has suffered dehydration, broken bones, snakebite, and countless other troubles on his trips—and usually comes up laughing. For the past two years, his highly popular column *Unbound* has appeared in *National Geographic Traveler* magazine.

What is it about travel that you love?

I've been addicted to travel since I was a kid. I read a book about Chinese political leaders and a book about a missionary's experience in New Guinea. I thought, I want to go to China and New Guinea to see what they're like for myself.

1 Probably a third of the time. When I worked for NBC News years ago, I traveled half the time or more. I was single then! Now I'm married with a family.

2 My kids have helped me to open my eyes and see things from a fresh angle. When my kids were younger, I gave one of them a camera and one a video camera. It was fun to compare their shots to my own and see how they saw things in a slightly different way.

3 I'm optimistic that people increasingly are aware that we have to do something, and I've seen small changes. Unfortunately, I've also seen places with serious damage. I've been to iconic, internationally famous spots where, just out of sight, they are dumping all the trash the tourists have left behind.

4 One of the greatest experiences of my life was the trip to Khumbu Icefall on Mount Everest. Unfortunately, while we were there, the best-known Sherpa climber in the world was killed. It shows that while travel is a lot of fun, there are risks involved sometimes. You have to be careful but enjoy it while you're there.

5 I want to go to new places in a way that gives me a better experience, not to go as an observer but as a participant. So I guess that is my philosophy of travel: Get off the tour bus.

1 Write the number of the paragraph (1–5) next to the question.

a Do you think we can avoid doing long-term damage to some of the great travel destinations?

b What is your most memorable travel experience?

c What have you learned from traveling with your children?

d How much time do you spend on the road in a typical year?

e What is your travel philosophy?

2 Read the interview again. Choose the correct option or options (a–c).

1 Boyd Matson travels _____.
   a in his work   b for pleasure
   c for family reasons

2 He became interested in traveling
   _____.
   a a long time ago   b recently
   c when he worked for NBC News

3 He thinks that travel is _____.
   a dangerous   b fun   c risky

4 When traveling, he prefers to _____.
   a experience new things
   b observe people
   c take part in things

Grammar present perfect and simple past

3 Look at the time expressions and complete the sentences about Boyd Matson with the present perfect and simple past form of the verbs.

1 Boyd Matson _____ (work) for National Geographic for years.

2 He _____ (write) hundreds of articles in his career.

3 He _____ (take) his kids to Machu Picchu a few years ago.

4 He _____ (not / have) any life-threatening experiences so far.

5 He _____ (have) an interesting time in Morocco last summer.

6 He _____ (be) on a working trip to Egypt this month.

5b Where to go, what to do there

Vocabulary vacation destinations

1 Complete the sentences from a travel agent's website with these words.

busy	crowded	exotic	peaceful	relaxing
remote	safe	tropical	unspoiled	vibrant

1 Explore the .... streets and .... markets of this .... city.

2 Get away from it all on a luxury break in .... surroundings.

3 Leave stress behind and recharge your batteries in the .... setting of a .... village high in the mountains.

4 Family-friendly vacations in .... resorts on the Mediterranean.

5 The vacation of a lifetime: .... beaches, ... scenery. Unforgettable.

6 Take a trip along the .... coastline of southern Australia.

Grammar present perfect continuous and present perfect, *How long … ?*

2 Complete the comments from visitors to the movie locations. Use the present perfect and the present perfect continuous forms of the verbs.

1 We .... (walk) around London all day—we .... (see) every Harry Potter site!

2 The guide .... (tell) us about the movie stars he .... (meet).

3 I .... (take) photos of this amazing scenery, but my battery .... (just / run out).

4 We .... (wait) for the weather to change so the balloon can take off—we .... (pay) for our tickets now, so I hope we can go up.

5 I .... (explore) Prague on my own. I .... (find) some lovely quiet corners.

6 Let's get a coffee. We .... (not / have) anything to drink and we .... (sightsee) since first thing this morning.

3 Rewrite the sentences using the words in parentheses. Use the present perfect or the present perfect continuous, as appropriate.

1 I came to the beach after breakfast. Now it's dinner time.
.... (lie / all day)

2 We set off at seven. It's now three o'clock.
.... (travel)

3 We first came here ten years ago. We come every year.
.... (come)

4 I started this book when I arrived. I haven't finished it yet.
.... (read)

5 I left Paris this morning. Now I'm in Rome.
.... (drive / 620 miles)

6 This is our third hotel this vacation!
.... (stay)

4 Write questions with *How long* and the present perfect continuous for sentences 1–4 in Exercise 3. Then write the answers.

1 ....

2 ....

3 ....

4 ....

5c The responsible traveler

Vocabulary conservation

1 Look at these words. Find and write:

eco-friendly	habitats	impact	issues
projects	species	waste	

1 two words that can follow:

  a conservation _____ ,
     conservation _____

  b threatened _____ ,
     threatened _____

2 words that mean the same as:

  a trash: _____

  b green: _____

  c effect: _____

Word focus *thing*

2 Match the statements (1–4) with the uses of the expressions with *thing* (a–d).

1 Andrew Marshall, an expert in all things green.

2 But I think the best thing is to use your common sense.

3 Tour operators have been taking steps to improve things in this area.

4 The thing is, there are lot of problems there.

a giving advice

b introducing a problem or explanation

c talking about general aspects of something

d referring to a group of unspecified ideas, objects, etc.

3 Complete the sentences with these expressions with *thing*.

a few things	and things	best thing
important thing	sort of thing	worst thing

1 I love visiting old churches _____ .

2 We're almost ready to go. I just need to take care of _____ .

3 The _____ about this trash is that it takes years to disappear.

4 She's really into conservation and that _____ .

5 The _____ about France is the food.

6 The _____ is to check with the tour operator.

Vocabulary review travel tips

4 Complete the travel tips with these words.

delays	local transportation	luggage	plan
around-the-world trip		travel	trip

TIPS FOR TRAVELERS

➤ ¹ _____ light—don't take unnecessary ² _____ .

➤ Relax—don't get stressed by ³ _____ .

➤ Use ⁴ _____ —it's cheaper and more fun.

➤ ⁵ _____ well and get the most from your ⁶ _____ .

➤ On an ⁷ _____ , it's often cheaper to fly east to west.

5 Complete the sentences with the correct form of *travel* or *trip*.

1 I just got back from a _____ to Greece.

2 We _____ across Australia by car.

3 I love going on long train _____ .

4 We went on a few day _____ from the resort.

5 How was your _____ ?

6 Air _____ is fast, but expensive.

Grammar review present perfect and simple past

6 Complete the conversation with the present perfect and simple past form of the verbs.

A: ¹ _____ you _____ (do) a lot of traveling?

B: Well, that depends what you mean by "a lot"! I ² _____ (go) to about six or seven countries, I suppose.

A: That's a lot! I ³ _____ (not / be) to that many. Where ⁴ _____ you _____ (go) on your last trip?

5d Is something wrong?

Vocabulary **travel problems**

1 Make compound nouns with these words.

allowance	pass	control	documents
car	poisoning	room	schedule

1 baggage _____
2 boarding _____
3 rental _____
4 food _____
5 hotel _____
6 passport _____
7 travel _____
8 train _____

2 Complete the sentences with the compound nouns from Exercise 1.

1 I forgot the _____ at home, so I hope the times are on our tickets.
2 You can't go back now—you've been through _____ .
3 Our _____ is right above the hotel kitchen!
4 Did they write the gate number on the _____ when we checked in?
5 We've had to pay extra because we went over our _____ .
6 I've got some medicine with me in case I get _____ .
7 Excuse me, where are the _____ offices? Are they outside?
8 Keep all your _____ in a safe place.

Real life **dealing with problems**

3 Match the comments (1–6) with the responses (a–f). Write T next to the things a tourist would say.

1 Can I help?
2 Why have we been waiting so long?
3 I wonder if you could help us?
4 Is there anything you can do about the air-conditioning?
5 I'm sorry, but I've lost the key to my room.
6 Is anything wrong?

a Don't worry. I'll give you another one.
b I hope so. It's about the noise from the room next door.
c I'll ask someone to take a look at it. Which room is it?
d Yes, I've left my bag with all my travel documents somewhere.
e Yes, of course. What's the problem?
f I'm afraid the flight has been delayed.

4 **Grammar review prepositions**

Complete the exchanges with these prepositions.

at	for	from

1 A: Which gate are you _____ ?
  B: I'm _____ gate 17.
2 A: Where have these people come _____ ?
  B: They're _____ the other bus—it broke down.
3 A: How long are you here _____ ?
  B: _____ another week.

5e Hello from Egypt!

Writing skill informal style

1 What do these informal expressions mean? Write them in the correct place.

> awesome   cool   no way   wow

1 I don't believe it / you. ....
2 I'm surprised. ....
3 I agree / approve. ....
4 That's incredible / amazing / impressive.
   ....

2 What do these abbreviations mean? Write them in the correct place.

> BTW   CM   LOL   oxox   thx

1 thank you: ....
2 hugs and kisses (to end a message): ....
3 laugh out loud (to say you found something funny): ....
4 by the way: ....
5 call me: ....

3 Add exclamation points to these sentences where appropriate.

1 The resort is fine.
2 The beach is beautiful.
3 The trip was exhausting.
4 I'm very tired.
5 I love it here.

4 Rewrite these sentences from a postcard as full sentences.

1 Food here delicious.
   ....
2 Been on a camel ride (bumpy!).
   ....
3 Never been so hot in my life!
   ....
4 Taking it easy today—did too much yesterday.
   ....
5 Photos in the usual place online.
   ....

5 Rewrite these sentences in a more informal style.

1 The weather here is great.
   ....
2 We've been lying by the hotel pool since we arrived.
   ....
3 I'm thinking of staying an extra week because it's so beautiful.
   ....
4 We've arranged to go on a couple of day trips.
   ....
5 We had a terrible flight. There was a long delay, the seats were uncomfortable, and there was no food!
   ....

6 Write a postcard from Egypt. Use the questions as a guide.

- What was the trip like?
- What's the weather like?
- What's the hotel like?
- What are the people like?
- What's the food like?

Wordbuilding **compound nouns (noun + noun)**

> ▶ **WORDBUILDING compound nouns (noun + noun)**
>
> We can use two nouns together to mean one thing.
> *baggage allowances*
> *boarding passes*
> Compound nouns can be made up of two words *(boarding pass)*, one word *(backpack)* or two words with a hyphen *(sky-diving)*. The plural is made by making the second noun plural *(hotel rooms*, not *hotels room)*.

1 Write the compound nouns in three groups.

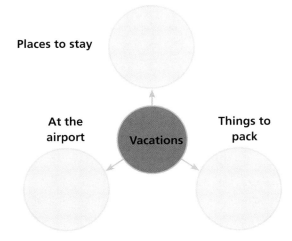

Places to stay

At the airport

Vacations

Things to pack

arrivals hall	carry-on luggage
baggage claim	insect repellent
budget hotel	money belt
campsite	sunscreen
departure lounge	youth hostel
guest house	

2 Write the names of these things.

1 You can wait to board the plane here:

2 Essential if you want to avoid itchy bites:

3 Inexpensive place to stay and not just for young people:

4 Not luxurious, and you need your own tent:

5 Where you pick up your luggage after leaving the plane:

6 You can take this on the plane:

7 A good idea if you are in dangerous areas:

8 Don't forget to put this on exposed areas of skin:

Learning skills **dictionary skills**

> A good dictionary gives you information about how a word is used as well as its meaning. This helps you to choose between confusing words.

3 Complete the dictionary definitions with the word they define: *travel* or *trip*.

> 1 _____ (n) (countable) the act of going somewhere and coming back again, usually for a short time *We've been on a day _____ to the capital.*
> 2 _____ (v) to go from one place to another, usually in a vehicle *We _____ by train a lot when we were in India.* (n) (uncountable) the activity of visiting different places *They say _____ is good for you.*

4 Find these words in your dictionary: *tour, trip,* and *voyage*. Then complete these sentences.

1 I've been on a sightseeing _____ around the island.

2 The _____ across the Indian Ocean took a couple of weeks.

3 What was the _____ to Paris like? Did you stop on the way?

4 I've been reading about James Cook's first _____ to the East.

Check!

5 Solve the anagrams to find words from Student Book Unit 5.

1 a d e l s y
you often get them at airports: _____

2 a c n v c a i t o e r s
people who are on a trip for pleasure, not work:
_____

3 a a b h i s t t
wildlife homes: _____

4 i m o o q s t u
be careful it doesn't bite you: _____

Unit 6 Wellbeing

6a Make it up

Word focus *make*

1 Read about two people discussing a cooking dilemma. Complete the sentences.

1 Are you going to ___make___ something?
2 Because it will help you to make _____
   _____ .
3 I still want to make _____
   _____ .
4 I could make cheese soufflé or chicken curry or just a _____ .
5 Can I make a _____ ?
6 All this talk about food is making _____
   _____ !

2 Add the expressions from Exercise 1 to the patterns (a–e).

a **make** (to produce something): *lunch, something,*
   _____

b **make** + noun (an action, to do something): *a plan, a mess,* _____

c **make** + *somebody* + noun (to do something for someone): *me a sandwich, you a snack,*
   _____

d **make** + *somebody* + adjective (to cause something): *me sick, you better,* _____

e other expressions: *make something up, make sense,*
   _____

3 Complete the sentences with expressions from Exercises 1 and 2.

1 I'm feeling stressed. I have to _____
   _____ for ten people today!
2 Look at the state of the kitchen! Why must you always _____ when you cook?
3 I can't eat much chocolate. It _____
   _____—it gives me a headache.
4 Are you thirsty? Can I _____
   _____ ?
5 I don't understand this recipe at all. It just doesn't _____ .
6 I'm hungry, but I can't _____
   _____ what to eat.

Grammar **modal verbs (1)**

4 Rewrite the visitor information from a national park with modal verbs. Sometimes more than one answer is possible.

> **1** Camping in the park is not allowed.
> **2** Picnics are restricted to designated areas.
> **3** Do not swim in the rivers.
> **4** It's a good idea to carry water with you.
> **5** Inform the rangers in advance of your visit.
> **6** It's not necessary to show identification on entry.
> **7** Approaching wild animals is not advisable.
> **8** Report any accidents or incidents with wild animals.

1 _____
2 _____
3 _____
4 _____
5 _____
6 _____
7 _____
8 _____

6b Strategies for success

Reading willpower

1 Read the statements about willpower.

Mental challenges are as difficult to pass as endurance tests. You pass through failure to success. You do not avoid failure. To me, the most exciting time is when things aren't going right. As a leader, you can't give up.

Robert D. Ballard, marine explorer

When I had to decide between the comfort of a staff news job and the risk of freelance photography, my mother told me that no great chasm was ever leaped in two small jumps.

Jodi Cobb, National Geographic *photographer*

People can build their willpower deliberately. We are born with a certain amount, but that is just a platform. I think you can build willpower and be strong and achieve a lot. Start with a step you feel comfortable with and take it one step ahead.

Børge Ousland, polar explorer

2 Match these missing sentences with the three quotes.

1 If you don't take a risk, you won't know what you're capable of.
2 You can develop your willpower if you want to.
3 If you give up, everyone will give up.

Grammar first conditional; *when, as soon as, unless, until, before*

3 Write complete sentences with the simple present and *will* + infinitive.

1 you make a healthy meal / feel better afterwards

2 I watch a movie / enjoy myself

3 you find a new route to work / save money

4 you take bottled water with you / not buy coffee

5 not buy chocolate / not eat it

6 live longer / have a good diet

4 Rewrite the sentences with the word in parentheses without changing the meaning.

1 You won't achieve anything if you don't take risks. (unless)

2 Your friends will help you if you ask them. (as soon as)

3 You'll be successful if you plan things carefully. (when)

4 You won't know what you can do if you don't try. (until)

5 You'll make a lot of mistakes and then you'll succeed. (before)

6 You won't save any money unless you have a plan. (if)

Vocabulary a healthy lifestyle

5 Which of these strategies are not part of a healthy lifestyle?

changing bad habits
cutting down on relaxation
avoiding outdoor activities
giving up junk food
cutting out fatty food

6c Alternative lifestyles

Vocabulary modern life

1 Circle the correct option to make things associated with a 24-hour society.

1 *electric* / *natural* light
2 *high* / *low* blood pressure
3 *outdoor* / *indoor* jobs
4 *day* / *night* work schedules
5 *irregular* / *regular* sleep

Reading alternative lifestyles

2 Read about Lisa Napoli and choose the correct option (a–c).

Radio journalist Lisa Napoli wanted to try and get away from the 24-hour lifestyle and so-called rat race of modern life. She was on a search for meaning in her life when someone suggested she head to Bhutan. No backpacker, Napoli went to Bhutan with a high-profile job—to help set up a new radio station. She fell in love with the country and even wrote a book, *Radio Shangri-La: What I Learned in Bhutan, the Happiest Kingdom on Earth*. In her book, Napoli describes how learning to live with less made her life richer. She explains that in Bhutan it was impossible to live a 24/7 lifestyle. So many people think they need and enjoy having a lot of stuff, but what if that's not possible? For Napoli, the key is to appreciate what is around you rather than to constantly desire and strive for things you do not have. If we value simplicity and respect the natural environment, we will be more content, she feels.

1 Lisa Napoli went to … .
 a Nepal
 b Tibet
 c Bhutan

2 She went there to … .
 a work
 b visit friends
 c go backpacking

3 As a result of her experience, she … .
 a became rich
 b learned to be content
 c gave up her job

3 Which statement(s) (a–c) agree(s) with what the presenter said?

a Napoli found she was happier with fewer material things.

b Napoli was not able to give up the 24-hour lifestyle.
c Napoli's experience is not applicable to anyone else.

4 Grammar extra **questions with *how***

a Look at the questions. What kind of word follows *How*?

1 How easy is it? ....
2 How quickly can we adapt to a different culture?
 ....
3 How determined do you have to be?
 ....
4 How realistic is it to make changes like this?
 ....
5 How did he manage? ....

b Write these words with the questions (1–6). Then match the questions with the answers (a–f).

badly	difficult	far	long	quickly	soon

1 How .... was it to give up money?
2 How .... is Bhutan from the United States?
3 How .... does it take to fly to Bhutan?
4 How .... did they do on the test?
5 How .... is the oil running out?
6 How .... can you get here?

a About ten hours.
b More than 1,800 miles.
c Disastrously!
d Give me an hour.
e It was quite easy, actually.
f That depends on which experts you believe.

6d Eating out

Vocabulary **restaurants**

1 Put the restaurant customer's words in order to make statements and questions.

1   from / that / made / what's

   .... ?

2   taste / they / like / what / do

   .... ?

3   I'll / think / that / try / I

   ....

4   come / does / with / vegetables / it

   .... ?

5   the / have / same / I'll

   ....

2 Grammar extra *need to*

> ▶ *NEED TO*
>
> We can use *need to* to say that it's important or necessary, rather than obligatory, to do something.
> *Is that restaurant busy at lunchtime? Do we need to make a reservation?*
>
> We can use *need to* when *have to* or *must* would sound too strong.
>
> *Don't need to* means it's not necessary to do something or that you can choose not to do it.
> *You don't need to have an appetizer if you don't want one.*

Complete the sentences with *need to* or *have to*.

1   Do we .... wait for the waiter to show us our table? (necessary)

2   You .... dress up—it's a pretty casual place. (not necessary)

3   It's formal—you .... wear a jacket and tie. (obligatory)

4   They don't accept reservations. You .... wait if it's busy. (obligatory)

5   You .... leave a tip—the service charge is included in the bill. (not necessary)

Real life **describing dishes**

3 Which is the odd word out in the sentences describing dishes?

1   It's like *potatoes / lamb / baked*.
2   They taste *salty / fish / spicy*.
3   It's made from *meat / vegetables / hot*.
4   It's a kind of *bland / boiled / fried* dish.

4 Read the comments. Is the person describing an appetizer (A), main course (M), or dessert (D)?

1   It's made of milk and it's quite sweet. It's usually served cold.

2   They're like little packages of vegetables. They're quite spicy.

3   It's a baked dish made from different kinds of meat and vegetables, with rice or pasta.

4   It tastes quite salty. It's a sort of spread for bread or toast.

6e A fitness center

Writing skill explaining consequences

1 Your local fitness center was remodeled recently and as part of this process there have been other changes. Look at the notes and write these headings in the correct spaces (1–3).

> cafeteria   opening times   prices

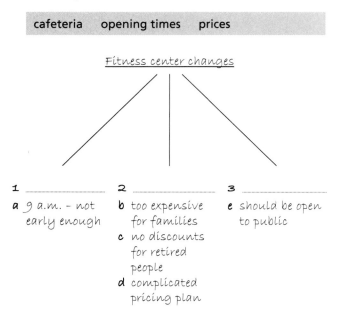

Fitness center changes

1 .... 2 .... 3 ....

a _9 a.m. – not early enough_

b _too expensive for families_

c _no discounts for retired people_

d _complicated pricing plan_

e _should be open to public_

2 Match the sentence halves. Then complete the sentences using these expressions for explaining consequences.

> Consequently   has led to   means that
> therefore   will result in

1 The swimming pool doesn't open until 9 a.m.,

2 Taking away the discounts for retired people

3 The pricing plan is too complicated.

4 Opening the cafeteria to the public

5 The price increase

a fewer families using the center now.
b people don't take advantage of offers.
c people can't go swimming before they go to work.
d they can't afford to use the center very often.
e more people using the center.

3 Use the information from Exercise 1 to complete this letter. Refer to the Student Book and Workbook Unit 4 to review formal style.

Dear Sir,

We are writing to express our concern about the recent changes to Newton Fitness Center. We are concerned about ....
....

In our view, ...
....
....

We also note that ....
....

In addition, ...
....

Finally, we feel that ....
....
....

We request that you review these changes to the services that the fitness center provides to local residents.

Sincerely

PH Singh

P.H. Singh
Newton Residents' Association

Wordbuilding
phrasal verbs

> ▶ **WORDBUILDING phrasal verbs**
>
> Phrasal verbs with *down* and *up* often describe change.
> *cut down*   *give up*

1 Complete the sentences with the correct form of these verbs and *up*.

go	grow	put	speed	take

1 The prices in the café have _____ since we were last here.

2 They've _____ some abstract paintings. It looks really different now.

3 I think I'll _____ cooking this winter.

4 If this bus doesn't _____ , we'll be late.

5 You should _____ and stop behaving like a child.

2 Complete the sentences with the correct form of these verbs and *down*.

bring	come	get	slow
take			

1 Strawberries are expensive now, but the price will _____ in the summer.

2 I'm on a diet because I have to _____ my weight _____ .

3 You'll have an accident unless you _____ .

4 We can't _____ these warning notices _____ —they have to be visible at all times.

5 There's a danger that the protests will _____ the government.

Learning skills planning writing

3 Look at the list of strategies for planning writing. Which strategies has this student used?

- noting the questions your writing needs to answer
- noting the purpose of your written text
- thinking about who the reader is
- brainstorming ideas
- brainstorming useful vocabulary or other language
- using a mind map to organize words
- organizing words in a table
- following a model text
- listing standard useful expressions
- listing useful linking words
- writing notes and short sentences
- organizing sentences by sequence or idea
- writing the same idea in different ways

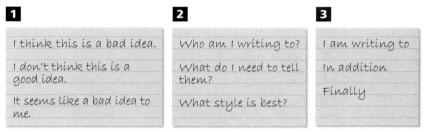

1
I think this is a bad idea.
I don't think this is a good idea.
It seems like a bad idea to me.

2
Who am I writing to?
What do I need to tell them?
What style is best?

3
I am writing to
In addition
Finally

4 Which of the strategies in Exercise 3 have you used when you have had to write something in English?

5 Answer the questions with reference to the writing you have done for the writing tasks in the Student Book and Workbook Units 1–6.

1 Which of the strategies did you use?

2 How helpful did you find them?

3 Is your writing more successful if you plan it first?

4 Which is the most useful strategy for you? Why?

Check!

6 Complete the crossword with the answers to the clues. All these words are in Student Book Unit 6.

1 A strong-smelling Asian fruit

2 Chips, candy, salty snacks, etc.

3 Something in food and drink that increases blood pressure

4 If food is not yet cooked, it's…

5 Another name for a savory banana

6, 7, 8 A cheese that has EU Guaranteed Traditional Speciality status

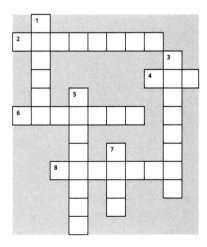

UNIT 1b, Exercise 9, page 13

Pair A: The Blue quiz
Ask Pair B the quiz questions without the options. Give them 5 points if they can answer the question immediately. Give them 1 point if they need to hear the options. The answer is in bold.

Pair B will then ask you the yellow questions.

1 Where do the Tuareg—or "blue people"—originally come from?
  a the Kalahari desert
  b the Namib desert
  c the Sahara desert
  They are an ethnic group in West Africa.
  The men traditionally wear blue.

2 Who lives in the Blue House in South Korea?
  a the president
  b the king
  c the prime minister
  It's the official residence and it has a blue-tiled roof.

3 What is the name of the country where the Blue Nile begins?
  a Sudan **b Ethiopia** c Uganda
  It originates in Lake Tana, then joins the White Nile to form the Nile river.

4 Which part of the US is famous for "the blues" (music)?
  a the West Coast
  b the Deep South
  c the Midwest
  The name comes from "the blue devils," meaning sadness and melancholy.

UNIT 3b, Exercise 10, page 37

Pair A
Read the solution to puzzle A. Pair B will ask you questions to solve it. Then ask Pair B questions to solve puzzle B.

> **Solution to puzzle A**
> The people on the yacht decided to have a diving competition. When they were all in the water, they discovered they had forgotten to put a ladder down the side of the yacht. They couldn't get back onto the yacht, so they drowned.

UNIT 8a, Exercise 11, page 95

Pair A
Decide what you think each photo shows. Then describe your photos to Pair B and find the correct captions.

1 What/Where could it be? Why?
2 What/Where can it not be? Why not?
3 What can you say for certain about the photo? Why?

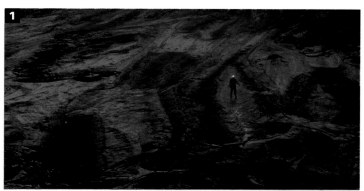

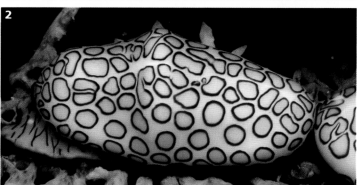

Two of these captions are for Pair B's photos. Listen to their descriptions of the photos and find the correct captions.

a A macro shot of a banana plant stem is magnified 32 times.
b A blue cod swims past sea pens—tiny animals which live in colonies shaped like branches.
c The space shuttle *Endeavour* lifts off from Cape Canaveral, Florida, leaving a trail of smoke.

UNIT 11a, Exercise 10, page 131

Pair A
Read the news story. Write a short dialogue between the man and a rescuer. Practice your dialogue so that you are ready to act it out for Pair B. Then turn back to page 131.

> A walker who got lost in the hills was rescued this weekend after taking a photo with his phone and emailing it to the Volunteer Rescue Service. The man had fallen and was injured, but with no maps he couldn't tell the rescuers where he was. He took the photo after advice from the rescue team, who then recognized his location immediately.

UNIT 1b, Exercise 9, page 13

Pair B: The Yellow quiz

Pair A will ask you the blue questions. You will get 5 points if you can answer the question immediately. You will get 1 point if you need to hear the options.

Then ask Pair A the yellow questions.

1 Which fruit does the California Yellow Fruit Festival celebrate?
   a the lemon
   b the pineapple
   c the banana
   Every September, Ventura County, California, holds a two-day lemon festival.

2 Which sport gives a yellow jersey to the winner?
   a golf
   b horse racing
   c cycling
   The Tour de France race takes place every year.

3 Where do yellow taxi cabs come from originally?
   a Chicago b New York c Washington
   Mr. Hertz started the Yellow Cab Company (in 1915) because yellow is the easiest color to see from a distance.

4 Where can you see the house that inspired Van Gogh's *Yellow House* painting?
   a Holland b Spain **c France**
   Van Gogh spent the summer of 1888 in Arles, in the south of France.

UNIT 3b, Exercise 10, page 37

Pair B

Ask Pair A questions to solve puzzle A. Then read the solution to puzzle B. Pair A will ask you questions to solve it.

> **Solution to puzzle B**
> The man had fallen into the Dead Sea. This is actually a saltwater lake. The salt density is so high that you can easily float on the surface.

UNIT 8a, Exercise 11, page 95

Pair B

Two of these captions are for Pair A's photos. Listen to their descriptions of the photos and find the correct captions.

a A man walks on cooled red lava at the Nyiragongo volcano in the Democratic Republic of the Congo.
b A man collects the salt after the water has evaporated from a stream in Peru.
c A flamingo tongue mollusc feeds on a blue-violet sea fan.

Decide what you think each photo shows. Then describe your photos to Pair A and find the correct captions.

1 What/Where could it be? Why?
2 What/Where can it not be? Why not?
3 What can you say for certain about the photo? Why?

UNIT 11a, Exercise 10, page 131

Pair B

Read the news story. Write a short dialogue between Adam and Corey. Practice your dialogue so that you are ready to act it out for Pair A. Then turn back to page 131.

> A message in a bottle which was put into the Atlantic Ocean in Florida has reached Ireland. Adam Flannery, aged 17, found the bottle which had been sent by high school student Corey Santos. The message gave Corey's contact details and asked the finder to get in touch with details of where the bottle ended up.

UNIT 4d, Ex 8, page 52

Student A: Choose a request (1–12). You are going to make this request.

Student B: Find the request for your partner's number. Choose an appropriate situation (a–d) for this request. You are going to respond to it.

Act out a conversation in this situation. Use the expressions for making and responding to requests on page 52 to help you. Take turns making and responding to requests.

Requests
1 You want to sit down.
2 You can't make out the phone number on a letter.
3 You don't know where the company buildings are.
4 You want an application form sent in the mail.
5 You need a pen.
6 You need a taxi.
7 You need to know the time.
8 You want help with an application form.
9 You need a ride somewhere.
10 You want to leave your coat somewhere.
11 You want to wash your hands.
12 You want to use the phone.

Situations
a You're with a friend.
b You're at a company's reception desk.
c You're in an interview.
d You're on the phone.

UNIT 5 Review, Exercise 8, page 68

Role 1
The most traveled airline pilot

Role 2
Wildlife conservationist of the year

Role 3
Writer of travel guides for independent travelers

UNIT 6 Review, Exercise 9, page 80

Baklava   A rich, sweet pastry with chopped nuts and syrup or honey. From Turkey, the Caucasus, and central Asia.

Borscht   A soup popular in many Eastern and Central European countries. Main ingredient: beetroot.

Couscous   From North Africa. A dish of semolina served with a meat or vegetable stew.

Curry   A south and southeastern Asian dish made with lamb, fish, or chicken on rice with a savory, spicy sauce.

Fondue   Popular in Switzerland and France originally. Pieces of bread are dipped into melted cheese.

Goulash   A Hungarian meat soup or stew, flavored with paprika.

Gravlax   Raw salmon cured in salt, sugar, and the herb dill. From Scandinavia.

Kebab   Cubes of meat (or fish) on a skewer, cooked over an open fire. Originally from Central and Western Asia.

Lasagna   A dish of pasta sheets layered with cheese, meat, and tomato sauce, and baked in the oven.

Pad thai   A stir-fried dish of rice noodles, scrambled eggs, peanuts, shrimp, and vegetables.

Paella   A rice dish originally from Valencia, Spain. Rice is cooked in a shallow dish with meat or seafood. Saffron flavors and colors the rice.

Tortilla   1 A type of flatbread made from corn or wheat in Central America.   2 A potato omelette from Spain.

Wontons   Chinese dumplings stuffed with ground pork, spices, and vegetables and usually fried.

UNIT 9b, Exercise 10, page 109

Work in two pairs within your group of four.

Pair A: Prepare a two-minute presentation on why it's better to buy famous brands. Give examples from your list in Exercise 10 on page 109.

Pair B: Prepare a two-minute presentation on why it's better to buy alternative brands. Give examples from your list in Exercise 10 on page 109.

Give your presentations to the class or to another group. Then take a class vote to find out how many people are going to try alternative brands.

UNIT 1
Simple present and present continuous
Form

Simple present

Affirmative	Negative
I/You/We/They **work**.	I/You/We/They **don't work**.
He/She/It **works**.	He/She/It **doesn't work**.

Interrogative	Short answer
Do I/you/we/they **work**?	Yes, I/you/we/they **do**. No, I/you/we/they **don't**.
Does he/she/it **work**?	Yes, he/she/it **does**. No, he/she/it **doesn't**.

Present continuous

Affirmative	Negative
I**'m working**. ('m = am)	I**'m not working**.
You**'re**/We**'re**/They**'re working**. ('re = are)	You/We/They **aren't working**. (aren't = are not)
He**'s**/She**'s**/It**'s working**. ('s = is)	He/She/It **isn't working**. (isn't = is not)

Interrogative	Short answer
Am I **working**?	Yes, I **am**. No, I**'m not**.
Are you/we/they **working**?	Yes, you/we/they **are**. No, you/we/they **aren't**.
Is he/she/it **working**?	Yes, he/she/it **is**. No, he/she/it **isn't**.

Use

We use the simple present to talk about:
- things that are always or generally true.
  Water freezes at 0° Celsius.
  Lucas doesn't paint portraits of people.
- things that are regular actions.
  Carla goes to an art class every Thursday.
  Does he go to the gym every day?
- permanent situations.
  He lives in Peru.
  They wear a uniform at work.

We use the present continuous to talk about:
- things that are in progress at the time of speaking.
  They're eating lunch now.
- temporary situations or situations happening "around now."
  I'm studying art at the moment.
- a situation that is in the process of change.
  People are wearing cheaper clothes nowadays.

Stative verbs

We usually use the simple present with stative verbs such as *like, love, hate, want, believe, know, sound, taste,* or *understand* to talk about states such as thoughts, senses, emotions, and possession. We don't usually use these verbs in the continuous form.
Isabel loves swimming.
He doesn't understand French.
Remember, some verbs can have both stative and dynamic meanings.
That guy looks great—I love his outfit!
Everyone is looking at him—he's wearing a great outfit!

We often use these time expressions with the simple present: *always, never, every day, on Mondays.* With the present continuous, we often use these time expressions: *at the moment, (right) now, this week, this summer.*

Practice

1 Complete the sentences with the simple present or present continuous form of the verbs.

1 They sometimes ___*work*___ (work) late.
2 _____ you _____ (want) to see the new color scheme for the office? It's red!
3 Irene _____ (study) Picasso's blue paintings at the moment.
4 I _____ (not like) that color at all!
5 It's fall and the trees _____ (change) color.
6 Tiger Woods is in the final round so he _____ (wear) his famous red shirt.
7 _____ Shui _____ (know) anything about South America?
8 This jewelry _____ (not come) from Africa. It's from Indonesia.

Question forms
Form

To form questions in the simple present we use *do* and *does* with the main verb.
Do you eat meat?
Does he usually work on Saturdays?

When we use a question word (like *what, where, who*) the question word comes in front of *do* and *does*.
What do they want to do?
Where does she study English?

We invert the subject and the verb when we make questions with *be* and modal verbs.
Are they in the kitchen?
Can she ride a bicycle?

When the question word is the subject of the question, we don't invert the subject and the verb.
Who likes this artist?
What is making that strange noise?

Common question words are: *who, what, when, where, why, how, which, how much/many.* You cannot form subject questions with *where, when, why,* or *how.*
Where do you live? (Not ~~Where you live?~~)
When does it start? (Not ~~When it starts?~~)

Use

We begin questions with *do/does, am/is/are, have/has,* and modal verbs when we want a *yes/no* answer, which is often very short.
***Does** he **live** in London? Yes, he does./No, he doesn't, but he is moving there soon.*
***Do** they **like** soccer? No, they don't.*
***Is** he in France now? No, he isn't./Yes, he's there until next week.*
***Can** they **come** on Monday? Yes, they can.*

We use question words when we want more information.
***When** does the bus arrive? It usually gets here at four o'clock.*
***Who** lives in that yellow house? Mr. Johnson lives there.*

Practice

2 Complete the questions.

1 *Where does* Ahmad *live?*
He lives in Dubai.
2 _____ they _____ to work?
They go to work by bike.
3 _____ the women always _____ in bright colors?
No, they don't. They only dress in bright colors at festivals.
4 _____ working?
No, I'm not. I'm checking my email.
5 _____ these lovely yellow flowers?
Susana bought them.
6 _____ I _____ to the movies tonight?
Yes, you can. What's playing?
7 _____ Nanoko always _____ that orange necklace?
She wears it because orange is the color of happiness. She's Japanese.
8 _____ blue shirts _____ Alex _____ ?
He has about twenty blue shirts.

UNIT 2
Present perfect
Form

We form the present perfect with the simple present of the verb *have* + past participle.

Affirmative	Negative
I've/You've/We've/They've **arrived.** ('ve = have)	I/You/We/They **haven't arrived.** (haven't = have not)
He's/She's/It's **arrived.** ('s = has)	He/She/It **hasn't arrived.** (hasn't = has not)

Interrogative	Short answer
Have I/you/we/they **arrived?**	Yes, I/you/we/they **have.** No, I/you/we/they **haven't.**
Has he/she/it **arrived?**	Yes, he/she/it **has.** No, he/she/it **hasn't.**

We add *-ed* to regular verbs to form the past participle: *arrive → arrived, work → worked, play → played, start → started.*
Note the spelling rules for other regular verbs:
- for verbs ending in *-e*, we add *-d: die → died, lie → lied*
- for verbs ending in *-y* (after a consonant), we change the *-y* to *i* and add *-ed: try → tried, study → studied*
- for verbs ending in vowel + consonant (not *-w, -x* or *-y*), we double the consonant: *stop → stopped, jog → jogged*

Some verbs have irregular past participles, for example: *do → done, find → found, have → had, know → known, make → made, meet → met*

Use

We use the present perfect:
- to talk about a situation that started at some time in the past and continues into the present.
*I **have played** in this band for three years.* (I am still playing in the band.)
- to talk about a past action with results in the present situation that we want to emphasize.
*They **have** recently **improved** this theater.* (The present situation is that the theater is better now.)
- to talk about situations in the past when there is no time reference given.
*Zap Mama **have had** several hits in Belgium.*
- when a time reference includes the present.
*We've **heard** a lot of great music **today**.*

When we are interested in a specific time in the past, we use the simple past:
*Zap Mama **had** several hits in Belgium **last year**.*

We use the present perfect with *since* and *for* to talk about how long a situation has continued. We use *since* with the point of time when the activity started, for example, *since Monday, since ten o'clock, since January, since I was a boy.*
*I've played the piano **since 2002**.*
We use *for* to talk about a period of time, like *for an hour, for three days, for two months, for a long time.*
*The band has played at the same festival **for five years**.*
Note that we do not use the simple present with *for* and *since* when the activity started in the past. We say:
He's been here since noon. (Not ~~He's here since noon.~~)

We often use the present perfect with *already, just,* and *yet* to talk about actions that happened recently, or actions that have not happened but we think will happen soon.
*I've **already** seen his new music video.*
*We've **just** been to see U2 in concert.*
*I haven't been to the opera **yet**, but I'd like to go one day.*

Practice

1 Complete the sentences with the present perfect form of the verbs, and choose *for* or *since*.

1 I *have worked* in this theater (for) / *since* twenty years. (work)
2 The band _____ this song at every concert *for* / *since* they started. (sing)
3 I _____ to the ballet *for* / *since* I was a child. (not be)
4 They _____ their own songs *for* / *since* many years. (write)
5 We _____ Eric Clapton play live *for* / *since* 2005. (not see)
6 The theater company _____ very hard *for* / *since* six months. (work)
7 _____ their manager _____ again *for* / *since* yesterday morning? (call)
8 Bob Dylan _____ the world continuously *for* / *since* many years. (tour)

Verb patterns: *-ing* form and infinitive
Form

-ing form	
verb + *-ing*	I **like playing** the violin.
-ing as the subject	**Playing** the guitar is magical.
preposition + *-ing*	They are **good at dancing**.

infinitive	
verb + infinitive	He **wants to play** the violin.
adjective + infinitive	This music is **easy to play**.

Use

We use the *-ing* form of the verb:
- after certain verbs such as *like, love, enjoy, prefer.*
  *I **love listening** to jazz.*
  Other verbs that are followed by the *-ing* form are: *can't help, consider, dislike, enjoy, finish, hate, imagine, involve, keep, mention, mind, don't mind, miss, postpone, practice, report, risk, stand, can't stand, suggest.*
- as the subject of the sentence: ***Dancing** is great exercise.*
- after a preposition: *I'm pretty quick **at learning** English.*

After certain verbs we use the infinitive form of another verb. This is often to talk about hopes, intentions, and decisions.
*He offered **to help** me.*
*They didn't want **to work** in the evening.*
Common verbs that are followed by an infinitive are: *afford, agree, aim, appear, arrange, attempt, can't bear, decide, demand, expect, hope, intend, learn, manage, need, offer, plan, prepare, promise, refuse, seem, want, wish, would like.*

Practice

2 Choose the correct option.

1 They like *to meet* / (*meeting*) new people.
2 That music is cheerful *to listen* / *listening* to.
3 We always enjoy *to see* / *seeing* good movies.
4 We want *to visit* / *visiting* the new art gallery.
5 *To act* / *Acting* in plays is very enjoyable.
6 Jose's really good at *to tell* / *telling* stories.
7 Do you need *to buy* / *buying* the tickets?
8 Penelope remembered *to be* / *being* on stage when she was a child—she was terrified!

UNIT 3
Simple past and past continuous
Form
Simple past

Affirmative	Negative
I/You/He/She/It/We/They **worked**.	I/You/He/She/It/We/They **didn't work**.

Interrogative	Short answer
Did I/you/he/she/it/we/they **work**?	Yes, I/you/he/she/it/we/they **did**.
	No, I/you/he/she/it/we/they **didn't**.

We add -ed to regular verbs to form the simple past: play → played, jump → jumped.

Note the spelling rules for other regular verbs:

- for verbs ending in -e, we add -d: realize → realized
- for verbs ending in -y, we change the -y to i and add -ed: carry → carried
- for verbs ending in vowel + consonant (not -w, -x, or -y), we double the consonant: plan → planned

Some verbs have an irregular affirmative form in the simple past:

do → did, go → went, see → saw

We use did and didn't to form questions and negatives.
Did you go fishing when you were at the beach?
Brad **didn't** swim in the pool yesterday.

Note that the simple past form of be is I/he/she/it was and we/you/they were. The negative forms are wasn't and weren't. We invert the subject and verb when we make questions.

Past continuous

We form the past continuous with the simple past of the verb be + the -ing form of the verb.

Affirmative	Negative
I/He/She/It **was working**.	I/He/She/It **wasn't working**. (wasn't = was not)
You/We/They **were working**.	You/We/They **weren't working**. (weren't = were not)

Interrogative	Short answer
Was I/he/she/it **working**?	Yes, I/he/she/it **was**. No, I/he/she/it **wasn't**.
Were you/we/they **working**?	Yes, you/we/they **were**. No, you/we/they **weren't**.

Use

Simple past

We use the simple past:

- to talk about a finished action in the past when there is a clear reference to a specific time or when the time is understood from the context. We often use a time phrase (yesterday, last week, ten years ago).
  I **visited** France last year.
  Did you **watch** the documentary yesterday?
- to describe a sequence of actions in a story.
  I **jumped** into the water and **swam** to the shore.
- for a single or repeated action in the past.
  I **went** to the lake. He **rode** the bus every day.

Past continuous

We use the past continuous:

- to describe an action in progress in the past. The past period (such as last week, last Monday) has finished.
  Last Friday we **were swimming** in the sea.

- to talk about an unfinished action in the past.
  I **was writing** a letter to my friend. (I probably didn't finish the letter.)
  I **wrote** a letter to my friend. (I finished the letter.)
- to describe a situation or the background to a story.
  The sun **was shining** in through the window.

Simple past and past continuous

We use the past continuous with the simple past to talk about two actions that happened at the same time in the past or when one action in progress (past continuous) was interrupted by another action (simple past). We can join the tenses with the words when, while, so, and because.

$$\text{time} \xrightarrow{\quad \overset{\textstyle \text{I met a group of tourists}}{\big\downarrow} \quad}$$
I was traveling through India

While I **was traveling** through India, I **met** a group of tourists.
What **were** you **doing** when you **heard** the news?
They **were enjoying** the boat trip, so they **didn't get off** the boat.

We can use when with both the simple past and the past continuous. We also often use while with the past continuous.

Remember, we don't use stative verbs (such as be, like, believe, understand) in the continuous form.

Questions in the past

- Questions in the past continuous ask about activities before an event: What **was** the crocodile **doing**? (before it started to come towards you)
- Questions in the simple past ask about activities after an event: Where did you go? (after you saw the crocodile)

Practice

1 Choose the correct option.

1. What was happening /(happened) after you fell / were falling in the water?
2. While Mateo swam / was swimming in the sea, a shark suddenly appeared / was appearing.
3. Kayley jogged / was jogging by the river when she lost / was losing her keys.
4. It didn't rain / wasn't raining, so they didn't take / weren't taking their raincoats.
5. It was / was being too hot to do anything, so everyone slept / was sleeping.
6. When we arrived / were arriving at the resort, the sun shone / was shining.
7. The girls surfed / were surfing when they saw / were seeing a dolphin.
8. Where was / did the crocodile swimming when you saw / were seeing it?

Past perfect

Form

We form the past perfect with the simple past of the verb *have* (*had*) + past participle.

Affirmative	Negative
I'**d**/You'**d**/He'**d**/She'**d**/It'**d**/We'**d**/They'**d watched**. ('d = had)	I/You/He/She/It/We/They **hadn't watched**. (hadn't = had not)

Interrogative	Short answer
Had I/you/he/she/it/we/they **watched**?	Yes, I/you/he/she/it/we/they **had**. No, I/you/he/she/it/we/they **hadn't**.

Use

We use the past perfect to talk about an event that took place before another event in the past that we have also related. We often use the past perfect and the simple past together.
*Jake **went** to the office yesterday after he **had met** his friends.* Jake met his friends before he went to the office.

	Jake met his friends	*Jake went to the office*	
time	↓	↓	→

We can use the following time expressions with the past perfect: *already, just, recently, before, previously, earlier, after,* and *by the time* to show the order in which the two past events happened.
*When Feng **got** to the theater, the movie **had already ended**.*
*He **had just returned** from the expedition.*
***After** I **had seen** them, I went back to the hotel.*
***By the time** we arrived, everyone **had left**.*

We use *because* and *so* to show that there is a reason for the later action.
*Feng was sad **because** he had missed the movie.*
*It had rained the night before, **so** he took his umbrella.*

When we relate past events in the same order they actually happened, we don't have to use the past perfect.
*I **got** up and then **went** to work.*

Practice

2 Complete the sentences with the simple past and the past perfect form of the verbs.

1 They ___had used___ (use) most of their air by the time they ___reached___ (reach) the wreck.
2 We _____ (pay) a deposit for the hotel before we _____ (buy) the train tickets.
3 The ship _____ (not arrive) in port by the time I _____ (wake) up.
4 The lake _____ (flood) because the snow _____ (melt).

5 Jim _____ (forget) her birthday, so his mother _____ (be) very angry.
6 The *Titanic* _____ (not reach) the US when it _____ (hit) an iceberg.
7 I _____ (sell) the yacht after I _____ (sail) around the world in it.

UNIT 4

Predictions

Form

Affirmative	Negative	Interrogative
I/you/he/she/it/we/they	I/you/he/she/it/we/they	
will	won't	will
could	couldn't	could
may	may not	may
might	might not	might
		I/you/he/she/it/we/they?

Use

We use *will, may, might, could* (*not*) + base form to make predictions about the future. We use *will* + base form to make predictions that we are certain about. The negative form is *won't*. We use *may, might,* and *could* + base form to talk about something we think is possible, but we are not certain. The negative forms are *may not, might not,* and *could not.*

*In ten years, China **will have** the world's largest economy.* (It's certain to happen.)
*In ten years, China **could have** the world's largest economy.* (China has the ability, but it's not certain that this will happen.)
*In ten years, China **may have** the world's largest economy.* (It's not clear that China has the ability so it's less certain this will happen.)
*In ten years, China **might have** the world's largest economy.* (It's possible, but far from certain.)

We can also use the adverbs *certainly, definitely, probably,* and *possibly* with *will* and *won't*. The adverbs describe whether we think something is more or less certain to happen.

	certainly/definitely	*probably*	*possibly*	
very certain				*not very certain*
	certainly not/ definitely not	*probably not*	*possibly not*	

When you use these adverbs with *will*, they come between *will* and the main verb. When you use the adverbs with *won't*, they come before *won't*.
*Next year, the US **will definitely have** the world's largest economy.* (I am sure it will.)

*In ten years, China **will probably have** the world's largest economy.* (I think it will, but I'm not certain.)
*Nepal **definitely won't have** the world's largest economy.* (I am sure it won't.)

Practice

1 Look at these predictions about the future. Put the word into the correct place in the sentence.

                    definitely
1 Earth's population will grow. (definitely)
2 We will pay to drive on all roads. (possibly)
3 It won't rain this afternoon. (probably)
4 People will live longer. (certainly)
5 Sea levels will rise. (definitely)
6 Life expectancy for people in the West will be 100 years. (possibly)
7 There will be more droughts. (probably)
8 Because of Internet shopping, there won't be as many stores. (definitely)

Future forms

Form

Present continuous: see also page 156
will: see also page 160

going to

Affirmative	Negative
I'**m going to** meet	I'**m not going to** meet
you'**re**/we'**re**/they'**re going to** meet	you/we/they **aren't going to** meet
he'**s**/she'**s** /it'**s going to** meet	he/she/it **isn't going to** meet

Interrogative	Short answer
Am I **going to** meet?	Yes, I **am**. No, I'**m not**.
Are you/we/they **going to** meet?	Yes, you/we/they **are**. No, you/we/they **aren't**.
is he/she/it **going to** meet?	Yes, he/she/it **is**. No, he/she/it **isn't**.

Use

We can use three different verb forms to talk about the future: present continuous, *will,* and *going to.*

Present continuous

We use the present continuous to talk about an arrangement at a specific (or understood) time in the future: *I'**m traveling** to Paris on Saturday morning.* (I already have my ticket.)

When we use the present continuous to talk about the future, we use a specified future time expression. If not, the present continuous refers to the present time.
We're working tomorrow. (= future)
We're working. (= present)

will

We use *will* to talk about something we decide at the moment of speaking.
*"Would you like another piece of cake?" "No, **I won't have** any more, thank you."*
We often use *will* with *I think…*
Now that I think of it, I will apply for the job.

going to

We use *be + going to + base form* to talk about a plan or intention for the future that has been decided before the moment of speaking.
*I'**m going to be** a lawyer.*

Practice

2 Choose the correct option.

1 (*We're leaving*)/ *We'll leave* / *We're going to leave* at three this afternoon. We've already booked a taxi.
2 *I'm buying* / *I'll buy* / *I'm going to buy* some sugar when I go into town.
3 Look at my sunburn! *I'm not spending* / *I won't spend* / *I'm not going to spend* so much time on the beach tomorrow!
4 I can't take the car on Monday. Paul *is taking* / *will take* / *is going to take* his driving test.
5 "Do you want anything to drink?" "Yes, *I'm having* / *I'll have* / *I'm going to have* fruit juice."
6 "I've got a terrible headache." "Just a minute, *I'm getting* / *I'll get* / *I'm going to get* you an aspirin."
7 "Why are you going to the supermarket?" "*I'm buying* / *I'll buy* / *I'm going to buy* some bread."
8 "When *are you flying* / *will you fly* / *are you going to fly* to Brazil?" "Next Monday."

UNIT 5

Present perfect and simple past

Form

Present perfect: see also page 157
Simple past: see also page 158

Use

We use the present perfect to talk about an experience when we don't say exactly when something happened. We use the simple past when we say, or it is clear from the context, when something happened in the past.
*I'**ve trekked** through Africa.* (I don't say exactly when.)
*I **trekked** through Africa last year.* (I say when.)

We often use the simple past after a present perfect question to give more specific information about an event or experience in the past.
Have you been to Rome?
Yes, I have. I went there in April 2011.

We use the present perfect with certain time expressions, for example: *already, just, yet, since, so far, this month, for, in the last five years.*
I've traveled a lot in the last five years.
They've already been to Egypt.
We use the simple past with specific times in the past, for example: *in 2011, yesterday, last summer, when I was a child, ago.*
I went on a round-the-world trip last year.
I saw a brown bear when I visited Canada.

Note that we can use *for* + period of time with both the present perfect and the simple past.
I've worked here for six months. (I still work here.)
I worked in Italy for twelve years. (I don't now.)

The verb *go* has two past participles: *been* and *gone.* We use *been* to say someone went somewhere and came back, and *gone* to say that they are still there.
Kim has been to the US. (She's not in the US now.)
Harry has gone to the US. (He's still there.)

Practice

1 Complete the conversation with the correct form of the verbs.

Paolo: Hi, James. [1] _____ (I / not see) you for a while. [2] _____ (you / be) away?

James: Hello, Pablo. Yes, [3] _____ (I / just / get back) from South America.

Paolo: Really? How long [4] _____ (you / be) there?

James: [5] _____ (I / spend) about a month there in total. You know how you lose some days just getting there and back!

Paolo: It sounds great. How many different places [6] _____ (you / get to)?

James: Oh, [7] _____ (I / go) to Bolivia, Chile, Peru, Brazil, and Venezuela.

Paolo: Lucky you! What about Patagonia? [8] _____ (I / hear) a lot about it.

James: No, that's in Argentina. [9] _____ (I / not / have) time. [10] _____ (it / be / too far).

Paolo: Well, maybe next time!

Present perfect continuous and present perfect / *How long… ?*

Form

Present perfect: see also page 157
We form the present perfect continuous with *have/has* + *been* + verb + *-ing.*

Affirmative	Negative
I've/You've/We've/They've **been waiting.** ('ve = have)	I/You/We/They **haven't been waiting.** (haven't = have not)
He's/She's/It's **been waiting.** ('s = has)	He/She/It **hasn't been waiting.** (hasn't = has not)

Interrogative	Short answer
Have I/you/we/they **been waiting?**	Yes, I/you/we/they **have.** No, I/you/we/they **haven't.**
Has he/she/it **been waiting?**	Yes, he/she/it **has.** No, he/she/it **hasn't.**

Use

We use the present perfect continuous to talk about recent continuous actions. It emphasizes the duration of an action.
I've been looking at the travel website all morning.
They haven't been traveling for long.
Has she been living here a long time?

We use the present perfect to emphasize the completion of a recent action, rather than the duration of the action. We also use the present perfect to talk about a specific number of times we have done something in the past, or the number of times we have produced or made something.
I've worked in several different countries.
We haven't heard from our friends in New Mexico since January.
She's been to Cambodia three times in the last year.
He's written five books.

We can use both the present perfect continuous and the present perfect to talk about the present result of a past action.
I've been working / I've worked all morning and I'm tired.

We use *How long… ?* + present perfect / present perfect continuous / simple past to ask about the duration of an activity.
How long have you had your bike?
How long have you been waiting?
How long did you stay in Chile?

Note that we don't usually use the present perfect continuous with stative verbs (like *be, have, know, like,* and *understand*).
I've known him for a long time. (Not *I've been knowing him for a long time.*)

Practice

2 Complete the conversations with the present perfect and continuous form of the verbs.

1. A: How long _have you been writing_ (you/ write) for a travel magazine?
   B: Ten years, and I _'ve visited_ (visit) 50 different countries.
2. A: She _____ (raise) $10,000 for charity.
   B: I know. She _____ (walk) for six weeks.
3. A: Tourists _____ (come) here for only ten years.
   B: Yes, but the number of tourists _____ (increase) a lot recently.
4. A: Edgar _____ (not travel) for long.
   B: No, but he _____ (see) lots of amazing sights already.
5. A: Did you know we _____ (complete) our diving instructor's course?
   B: Really? How long _____ (you/train)?

UNIT 6

Modal verbs (1)

Form

Affirmative	Negative	Interrogative
I/you/we/they have to he/she/it has to	I/you/we/they don't have to he/she/it doesn't have to	Do I/you/we/they have to? Does he/she/it have to?
I/you/he/she/it/we/they can must should	I/you/he/she/it/we/they can't (= cannot) mustn't (= must not) shouldn't (= should not)	can must should I/you/he/she/it/we/they?
I'm allowed to you're/we're/they're allowed to he's/she's/it's allowed to	I'm not allowed to you/we/they aren't allowed to he/she/it isn't allowed to	am I allowed to? are you/we/they allowed to? is he/she/it allowed to?

Note these rules for modal verbs (like *can, must, should*):

- There is no third person *-s*. She **must** go. I **can** stay.
- There is no auxiliary *do*. He **can't** play.
- There is no *to* before the verb. He **should** be here.

The expression *have to* is not technically a modal verb as it does take a third person *-s*, but it is used to express obligation like the modal *must*.

Use

We use modal verbs to talk about what is allowed:
- We use *have to / has to* and *must* to say if something is obligatory.
  You **have to / must** *follow the recipe.*
- We use *don't/doesn't have to* to show that something is not important or necessary.
  He **doesn't have to** *go to work on Saturday.*
- We use *can* and *is/are allowed to* to talk about permission.
  We **can / are allowed to** *eat our lunch here.*
- We use *can't* and *isn't/aren't allowed to* to say if we don't have permission or it's important not to do something.
  You **can't / aren't allowed to** *bring your own food.*
- We use *should/shouldn't* to make a recommendation or give advice.
  You **shouldn't** *eat raw seafood.*

Note the difference between *have to* and *must* in the negative.
You **don't have to** *eat it.* (It is not obligatory.)
You **must not** *be late.* (It's important.)

Practice

1 Complete the sentences with the correct modal verbs.

1. You _shouldn't_ eat before you go swimming. (recommendation)
2. You _____ cook chicken thoroughly before eating it. (obligation)
3. You _____ eat in the classroom. (no permission)
4. He _____ tell anybody about our new menu. (prohibition)
5. This is an informal restaurant. You _____ wear a uniform. (no obligation)
6. You _____ eat five servings of fruit and vegetables every day. (recommendation)
7. They _____ have one small snack between meals. (permission)
8. I _____ remember to take my vitamin pills today. (obligation)

First conditional

Form

We form the first conditional using:
If + simple present, will + base form
*If you **make** a plan, you **will succeed**.*
*You **won't lose** weight **if** you **eat** a lot of junk food.*
We can use *if* in two positions:
- If-clause first: *If you believe in yourself, you will achieve your dream.*
- Main clause first: *You will achieve your dream if you believe in yourself.*

When the *if*-clause is at the beginning of the sentence, we use a comma to separate it from the main clause.

Use

We use the first conditional to talk about a possible future action or situation. We can also use it to talk about things that are generally true.
If you take up a new sport, you'll get in better shape.
If you eat fatty foods, you won't be healthy.

We can also use *when, as soon as, unless, until,* and *before* instead of *if* to talk about situations in the future. We use the present tense after *if, when, as soon as, unless, until,* and *before* when we refer to future events.
***When** the rain stops, we'll have a picnic.*
*You won't get thinner **unless** you give up sugar.* (= You won't get thinner if you don't give up sugar.)
***As soon as** lunch is ready, they will eat.*
*We won't eat lunch **until** it's ready.*
*We won't pick the apples **before** they are ripe.*

Practice

2 Complete the sentences with the simple present and *will* + base form.

1 I ___will make___ (make) this meal at home if they ___show___ (show) me how to cook it.
2 If you _____ (recommend) the CD, we _____ (buy) it.
3 When the sun _____ (come) out again, we _____ (feel) much better.
4 You _____ (get) a stomachache unless you _____ (eat) more slowly.
5 We _____ (not eat) chocolate until we _____ (lose) weight.
6 As soon as we _____ (get) home, we _____ (do) some exercise.
7 I _____ (not change) my diet until I _____ (see) the doctor.
8 We _____ (do) some warm-up exercises before we _____ (do) aerobics.

UNIT 7

Comparatives and superlatives

Form

Adjective/Adverb	Comparative	Superlative
short adjective/adverb		
warm	warmer (than) less warm (than) (not) as warm as	(the) warmest
fast	faster (than) less fast (than) (not) as fast as	(the) fastest
long adjective/adverb		
interesting	more interesting (than) less interesting (than) (not) as interesting as	(the) most interesting
quickly	more quickly (than) less quickly (than) (not) as quickly as	(the) most quickly
irregular adjective/adverb		
good (adj) well (adv)	better	(the) best
bad (adj) badly (adv)	worse	(the) worst

We add *-er* to regular short adjectives and adverbs to form the comparative, and we add *-est* to regular short adjectives and adverbs to form the superlative: *warm → warm**er** → warm**est**; fast → fast**er** → fast**est***
We add *more/less* and *most* to form the comparative and superlative forms with longer adjectives and adverbs: *interesting → **more** interesting → **most** interesting; quickly → **more** quickly → **most** quickly*
Note the spelling rules for comparative and superlative adjectives and adverbs:
- for adjectives and adverbs ending in *-e*, add *-r/-st*: *large → larg**er** → larg**est***
- for adjectives and adverbs ending in *-y* (after a consonant), change the *-y* to *–i* and add *-er/-est*: *easy → eas**ier** → eas**iest***
- for adjectives and adverbs ending in consonant–vowel–consonant, double the final consonant and add *-er/-est*: *big → big**ger** → big**gest**; hot → hot**ter** → hot**test***

Use

We use comparative adjectives and adverbs to compare two things. We use *than* after a comparative adjective/adverb.
*My apartment is **smaller than** your apartment.*
*This car is **less expensive than** that car.*
*Daniel can run **more quickly than** Amelie.*

We use *as…as* to compare two things that are the same or equal. We use *not as…as* to say they aren't the same or equal.
*This tent is **as** warm **as** a trailer.*
*The oil stove **doesn't** work **as** efficiently **as** a gas stove.*

We use superlative adjectives and adverbs to compare three or more things. We usually use *the* before a superlative adjective.

*People say it's **the most expensive** house in the world.*
*Airplanes are **the fastest** form of transportation.*

We use modifiers such as *a bit, a little,* and *slightly* before comparative adjectives and adverbs to talk about small differences, and *a lot, much,* and *far* to talk about large differences.

*My car is **slightly** newer than yours.*
*Electric cars are **much** more expensive than gas cars.*

Common expressions with comparative forms are:
- *the* + comparative, *the* + comparative.
  The bigger the engine, **the faster** you go.
  The quicker we leave, **the sooner** we'll get there.
  The bigger they are, the **harder** they fall.
- *get* + comparative + *and* + comparative.
  It's **getting easier and easier** to build your own house.
  They got **more and more tired** as the day went on.

Practice

1 Choose the correct option.

1 This apartment *is bigger than / isn't as big as* that huge house.
2 Salech runs *fastest / as fast as* Abdul.
3 Their house is *the biggest / as big* I have ever seen!
4 This car is a little *most expensive / less expensive* than that one.
5 This yurt is much *more warm / warmer* than the tent we stayed in last year.
6 The weather is getting hotter and *more hot / hotter.*
7 Her kitchen is *smaller than / smallest* mine.
8 The *quickest / quicker* we get home, the sooner we'll get some news.

used to, would, and the simple past
Form

Affirmative	Negative
I/you/he/she/it/we/they **used to** **would**	I/you/he/she/it/we/they **didn't use to** **wouldn't**

Interrogative	Short answer
Did I/you/he/she/it/we/they **use to?**	Yes, I/you/he/she/it/we/they **did.** No, I/you/he/she/it/we/they **didn't.**
Would I/you/he/she/it/we/they?	Yes, I/you/he/she/it/we/they **would.** No, I/you/he/she/it/we/they **wouldn't.**

We use the base form after *used to* and *would*. Note that the negative and question forms of *used to* do not have a final -*d*:

*Sophie **didn't use to** like opera. **Did** you **use to** like it?*

Simple past: see also page 158

Use

We use *used to* to talk about a situation, a state, or a habit in the past.

*I **used to** drive to work before they opened the subway.*
***Did you use to** go on vacation with your family?*

We can also use *would* to talk about past habits, but not about past states or situations.

Habit: *We **would** go out every Saturday evening.*
State/Situation: *We **used to** live in the country. We **didn't use to** have a car.*

We don't use *used to* or *would* with a specific time in the past. We use the simple past instead.

I used to go to college ~~in 2009~~.
I went to college in 2009.

We can only use *used to* to talk about the past. We cannot use it to talk about the present.

*I **used to go** to the park every week. (past)*
*I **usually go** to the park every week. (present)*

Practice

2 Complete the sentences with *used to* and the verbs. In which of the sentences can you also use *would*?

1 I *used to live* (live) in San Francisco when I was young.
2 They _____ (not have) their own house.
3 _____ there _____ (be) more forests and parks in the city?
4 The boys often _____ (play) tennis in the park.
5 Where _____ your father _____ (work) when he was younger?
6 She _____ (not go) to the movies often when she was a girl.
7 He _____ (tell) me all about his life in Australia.
8 We _____ (eat) lunch in a café near my grandparents' house.

UNIT 8

Modal verbs (2)

Form

Affirmative	Negative	Interrogative
I/you/he/she/it/we/they	I/you/he/she/it/we/they	
must	must not	must
might	might not	might
may	may not	may
could	couldn't	could
-	can't	can I/you/he/she/it/we/they?

must / might (not) / may (not) / could / can't + base form
It **must be** the original painting.
The animals **may not return** before sunset.
It **could be** a butterfly egg.
The colors **can't be** real.

must / might (not) / may (not) / could / can't + be + *-ing*
They **must be waiting** for spring.
The birds **could be looking** for a place to nest.
She **can't be using** that camera—it's not digital.

Rules for modal verbs: see also page 163

Use

We can use *must / might (not) / may (not) / could* and *can't* + base form or *be + -ing* to speculate and deduce things about present situations. We make the deduction based on some form of evidence.

We use *must* when we are certain something is true.
The nest **must be** somewhere nearby. (There is evidence for this, for example: *We've seen the birds.*)
She **must be telling** the truth. (We believe that she wouldn't normally lie.)

We use *might, may,* or *could* to say that we think it's possible something is true, but we aren't certain.
He **might be** right about it.
Their natural habitat **may be changing**.
Your plan **could work**.

We use *might not* and *may not* to say that we think it's possible something is not true.
We **might not find** the road before dark.
They **may not be looking** for us now.

We use *can't* when we are certain that something is not true.
That **can't be** the truth.
We **can't be going** in the right direction.

Practice

1 Complete the sentences with *must, may, might not, could,* or *can't* and the correct form of the verbs (base form or *be + -ing*).

1 It ___must be___ (be) a burial site. There's evidence of human remains.
2 This _____ (be) a new species, but I need more evidence.
3 This was their nest but the birds _____ (live) here any more. It's empty.
4 They _____ (have) some good photos, but I don't think so.
5 They _____ (recognize) this place; they come here every year.
6 It's only got six legs, so it _____ (be) a spider.
7 The aurora borealis is unpredictable _____ so we (see) any lights tonight.
8 The trees are turning yellow. Fall _____ (come).

Modal verbs (3)

Form

must / might (not) / may (not) / could / can't + have + past participle
It **must have been** amazing.
They **might have seen** this before.
It **could have been** the original painting.
The colors **can't have been** real.

Use

We can use *must / might / may / could / can't* and *could + have* + past participle to speculate and deduce things about the past. We often make the deduction based on some form of information or evidence.

We use *must have* + past participle when we are certain that something was true.
People **must have lived** in this valley for thousands of years.

We use *might / may / could have* + past participle when we think it's possible something was true, but we aren't certain.
They **might have made** boats from these trees, but we haven't found any.
These people **could have eaten** fish, but there are no rivers near here.
People **may have cooked** food, but there isn't any evidence of fires.

We use *can't/couldn't have* + past participle when we are certain that something wasn't true.
They **can't have used** carts. They hadn't been invented.
I **couldn't have gone** because I was sick.

Practice

2 Choose the correct option.

1 They *must have /* *can't have* lived in the trees—they couldn't climb.
2 They *can't have / may have* been able to write—these look like a kind of old pencil.
3 They *must have / couldn't have* collected fruit because there are seeds and skins here.
4 These people *can't have / might have* ridden horses, but I'm not sure.
5 The hunters *couldn't have / must have* killed elephants—they are too big.
6 They *can't have / might have* kept rabbits as pets but I think they ate them.
7 They *can't have / may have* used metal knives—they only used stone tools.
8 They *must have / could have* worn cotton clothes, but we believe they wore leather.

UNIT 9

Noun phrases

Form

a / an + singular count noun
*He got **a** credit card bill for $500.*
*I'd like to give you **an** example of a successful bank.*

the + singular and plural count nouns, noncount noun
*Have you paid **the** bill that arrived yesterday?*
*She was having difficulty making **the** mortgage payments.*
*He made **the** bed.*

zero article + plural count noun, noncount noun
*I like watching **American movies**.*
*I love **pasta**.*

possessive adjectives: *my, your, his, her, its, our, their* + noun
*I can send **my** bank emails or text messages.*
*How do you pay **your** household bills?*

Determiners

each/every + singular count noun
***Every** customer gets a free sample.*
*I always check **each** bank statement before I file it.*

all + plural noun
*They don't treat **all** customers the same way.*

all + *the* + noun (plural count and noncount) and *all* + *of* + *the* + noun.
*We interviewed **all the** people who came into the store.*
*There are sales in **all of the** stores at the moment.*

Use

Articles in noun phrases

We use *a / an* + singular count noun:
- to say that a person or thing is one of many. *He's **a** bank manager.* (There are lots of them.)
- to refer to a person or thing for the first time. *There's **a** new cell phone store in town.*
- to talk about a person or a thing in general. *I'm looking for **a** new job.*

We use *an* with singular count nouns that start with a vowel: *You will receive **an** email.*

We use *the* + singular or plural count noun or noncount noun:
- to say there is only one of this thing. *He's **the** director of the new shopping mall.*
- to refer back to the same thing or person for a second time. *Those are **the** shoes I wanted to buy.*
- with certain countries, place names, geographical regions, oceans and seas, deserts, mountain ranges, and rivers, for example: *the US, the UK, the Philippines, the Eiffel Tower, the White House, the Middle East, the Antarctic, the Pacific, the Mediterranean, the Kalahari Desert, the Alps, the Himalayas, the Amazon, the Nile.*
- with superlative adjectives, for example: *the biggest city, the newest store, the most expensive phone.*
- when there is only one, for example: *the world.*

We use zero article + plural count noun and noncount noun to refer in general to people, animals, or things.
*I don't receive **bank statements** by mail anymore.*
***Online banking** is very convenient.*
*Do you like **cats**?*

We do not use *the* with the names of people, towns, countries, continents, lakes and mountains, languages, for example: *Christopher Columbus, New York, Beijing, Australia, Poland, China, Africa, Europe, Lake Titicaca, Mount Everest, English, Spanish, Japanese.*

Determiners and possessives in noun phrases

We use determiners and possessives in front of nouns to make the information about them more specific.

We use possessive adjectives: *my, your, his, her, its, our, their* + noun to express ownership and possession.
*Where is **my** credit card? This isn't **your** mobile phone.*

We use the determiners *each* and *every* with singular count nouns to refer to individual things.
*They had to pay **every** bill before they moved out.*
***Every store** was full.*

We use the determiner *all* with plural count nouns to refer to a group of things.
*Discounts are available in **all** the local stores this week.*
*There are mortgage offers in **all** the banks right now.*

Practice

1 Complete the sentences with these words. Two sentences are already complete.

| a | all | an | every | the | your |

1 Do you have any money in _____ savings account?
2 There's a free gift with _____ new cell phone subscription.
3 Where is _____ money I gave you last night?
4 Do you think _____ stores are good places to work in?
5 Would _____ staff members please report to the manager after work?
6 Jan had _____ idea about how to spend the money we had won.
7 The price of _____ gas has gone up again.
8 It's _____ sunny day.

Passive voice: all tenses

Form

We form the passive with the verb *be* + past participle.

Tense	Active	Passive
Simple present	makes/make	**is/are** made
Present continuous	is/are making	**is/are being** made
Simple past	made	**was/were** made
Past continuous	was/were making	**was/were being** made
Present perfect	has/have made	**has/have been** made
can	can make	**can be** made
will	will make	**will be** made

Use

We use the passive voice when we want to focus on an action or the object of the action, rather than the person who is doing the action. The object of the active sentence becomes the subject of the passive sentence.

      subject   object
Active: *The workers carry the boxes.*
        subject   object
Passive: *The boxes are carried by the workers.*

In a passive sentence, we can say who did the action (the agent) using *by*. We use *by* + agent when it is important to know who did the action. It isn't always necessary to use *by* + agent. We don't usually mention the agent when it is obvious who has done the action, when we don't know, or when it isn't important.
Bananas are grown in Costa Rica by farmers.

Practice

2 Rewrite the sentences in the passive form. Use *by* + agent where appropriate.

1 They will transport the goods to Asia by ship.
   The goods will be transported to Asia by ship.
2 Rashid bought a car last month.

3 Will they build a new factory to create new jobs?

4 They are producing fair-trade crafts in this village now.

5 Were they making MP3 players last year?

6 The company can't complete the project in less than two years.

7 People will not buy so many goods next year.

8 They have sold Borders Books to B&N to raise money.

UNIT 10

Defining relative clauses

Form

He is the man ***who (that)*** *invented the World Wide Web.*
This is the system ***which (that)*** *I told you about.*
That is the place ***where*** *we buy our computers.*

The relative pronouns *who, which, whose, where, when,* and *that* introduce defining relative clauses.

Relative pronoun	Gives information about	Example sentence
who	people	He's the doctor **who** treated all those children.
which	things	That's the jeep **which** can cross the desert easily.
where	places	This is the beach **where** they do extreme surfing.
whose	possessions	She's the runner **whose** leg was broken in three places.
when	time	This weekend is **when** the marathon takes place.
that	people	There's the man **that** ran 1,000 kilometers last week.
	things	These are the shoes **that** he wore to run 1,000 kilometers.

Use

We use defining relative clauses to give us essential information about a person, thing, place, possession, or time.
*That's the doctor **who** carries out the transplants.*
*Cosmetic surgery is a process **which/that** can restore faces.*
*This is the hospital **where** you go for help.*
*That's the surgeon **whose** procedure we use.*
*1992 is the year **when** Dr. Alvarez got his degree.*

We can use *that* for people or things instead of *who* or *which*. This is less formal.
*The person **that** discovered the solution was from China.*
*The factory **that** produces it employs 200 people.*

We always use *who, which,* and *that* when it is the **subject** of the defining relative clause (that is, when those relative pronouns are followed by the verb).
*He's the man **who** did the first bungee jump.*
*Is this the device **that** replaces a damaged hip?*

We can leave out *who, which,* and *that* when they are the **object** of the relative clause (that is, when they are followed by a noun or a pronoun).
*He's the man (**who**) I met in New Zealand.*
*That's the operation (**that**) she had last year.*

Practice

1 Write sentences using *who, which, where, whose,* and *when*. In which sentences can you use *that*? In which sentence can you leave out the relative pronoun?

1 this is the machine / it makes new body parts
   This is the machine which (that) makes new body parts.

2 there's the man / he flew around the world alone

3 that's the cave / four explorers slept there

4 she's the girl / her arm was operated on

5 it's the time of day / the helpline is busiest

6 here is the boat / they crossed the Atlantic in

7 this is the woman / she climbed Everest

8 we saw the device / it treats headaches

Second conditional

Form

We form the second conditional using:
If + simple past, would + base form
***If** you **introduced** oxygen, plants **would grow**.*
*Rain **wouldn't fall if** the temperature **stayed** the same.*

We can use *if* in two positions:
• If-clause first: *If you tried, you would win.*
• Main clause first: *You would win if you tried.*
When the *if*-clause is at the beginning of the sentence, we use a comma to separate it from the main clause.

We can also form the second conditional with *could* and *might* instead of *would*:
*If there was soil, plants **could** be introduced.*
*If oxygen was introduced, forests **might** grow.*

Note that the contracted form of *would* is *'d*. Don't confuse the contracted forms of *would* (*'d*) and *had* (*'d*).
*They**'d** go on more space exploration if it was less expensive.* (= They **would** go)
*They**'d** gone to the moon years ago.* (= They **had** gone)

Use

We use the second conditional to talk about imagined situations in the present or future that are:
• possible but not probable.
   *If I **had** a lot of money, I **would** buy a Ferrari.* (I don't think it's very probable this will happen.)
• impossible.
   *If I **was** French, I**'d understand** this movie.* (But I'm not French.)
Note that when we use the simple past with *if*, it refers to the present or future, not the past.

We often use *If I were you* rather than *If I was you*, especially when giving advice.
If I were you, I'd train to be a scientist.

Practice

2 Complete the sentences with the simple past and *would* + base form.

1 If he ___*won*___ (win) the competition, he ___*would be*___ (be) very happy.
2 If she _____ (pass) her exams, I'm sure she _____ (go) to more concerts.
3 He _____ (not have) cosmetic surgery if he _____ (not need) it.
4 _____ you _____ (live) on Mars if you _____ (have) the chance?
5 If the boys _____ (like) music, they _____ (go) to more concerts.
6 _____ humans _____ (change) Mars if they really _____ (want) to?
7 If you _____ (have) the opportunity to travel into space, _____ you _____ (take) it?
8 If I _____ (be) you, I _____ (rest) before the journey.

UNIT 11

Reported speech

Form

When we report what someone said, we often move the tense "backwards."

Direct speech	Reported speech
Simple present Maria: "I **live** in Peru."	*Simple past* Maria said (that) she **lived** in Peru.
Present continuous James: "I **am working** at home."	*Past continuous* James said (that) he **was working** at home.
Simple past Vikram: "The interpreter **left** this morning."	*Past perfect* Vikram said (that) the interpreter **had left** that morning.
Past continuous Ali: "We **were working** here."	*Past perfect continuous* Ali said (that) they **had been working** there.
Present perfect Katy: "I **have never been** to Africa."	*Past perfect* Katy said (that) she **had never been** to Africa.
will/won't Lin: "I **won't visit** them."	*would/wouldn't* Lin said (that) he **wouldn't visit** them.
can/can't Eugenia: "I **can't do** it."	*could/couldn't* Eugenia said (that) she **couldn't do** it.

We often make other changes in reported speech:
- Pronouns: *I → he/she; we → they; my → his/her; our → their; you (object) → me*
- Time expressions: *now → then; today → that day; tomorrow → the next day; yesterday → the previous day; last night → the night before; this morning → that morning*
- Other changes: *this → that; here → there*

Reported questions

For *yes/no* questions, we form reported questions using *if* or *whether*. We do not use the auxiliary verb *do* in the reported question.
"Do you want to work on this project?" → He asked (me) **if/whether I wanted to work** on that project.

When we report questions with *what, why, where, who, when,* and *how,* the word order in the reported question is the same as for an affirmative statement.
"What have you been doing?" → I asked (him) **what he had been doing**.
"Why haven't we seen this information before?" → She asked **why they hadn't seen** that information before.
We do not use question marks in reported questions.

Use

We use reported speech to report someone's words from the past.
Direct speech: *"The photos are on YouTube."*
Reported speech: *She said (that) the photos were on YouTube.*

Note that there is no difference whether we use or don't use the conjunction *that*.

We can also report questions in the past.
Direct speech: *"What are you doing?"*
Reported speech: *I asked what he was doing.*

Direct speech: *"Do you think this policy will work?"*
Reported speech: *He asked if I thought the policy would work.*

Common verbs for reporting what people have said are: *say, tell, explain, suggest, think, recall.*

Note that we don't follow *say* with an object.
"I think we'll go."
Sue **said** (that) she thought they would go.
However, *tell* always needs an object.
"I think we'll go."
Sue **told me** (that) she thought they would go.

Practice

1 Change the direct speech into reported speech. Remember to make changes to pronouns and time expressions where necessary.

1 Greg: "I have a new digital camera."
   Greg said that he had a new digital camera.

2 Anita: "I'll read the news report tomorrow."

3 Joe: "I visited the Amazon rain forest on my trip to South America last year."

4 Mai: "Can I give you a donation for charity?"

5 Nasrin: "I've just seen the documentary about endangered languages of the world."

6 Miguel: "I was reading the paper yesterday."

7 Simon: "Have you ever met anyone from Peru?"

8 Manuela: "We're meeting at nine tomorrow."

Reporting verbs

Form

ask / tell / remind / invite + someone + (*not*) *to* + base form
*The manager **asked** his employees **to turn off** their cell phones at work.*
*She **told** me **to finish** the report by the end of the day.*
*Jaime **reminded** his friends **to update** their software.*
*We **invited** our clients **to attend** the opening party.*

promise / offer + (*not*) *to* + base form
*They **promised** **not to blog** about the incident.*
*She **offered to send** a text about the party.*

The reporting verbs *realize, think, wonder,* and *know* have the same pattern as *say* and *ask* (see Reported speech on page 170).
She realized (that) she had forgotten to turn off her cell.
They knew (that) she was coming to visit on the weekend.
Feng wondered if they read his blog.

Use

Say, tell, and *think* are the most common reporting verbs, but we often use others to report speech.
"Please check your information before continuing." → *The website **reminded** customers to check their information before continuing.*
"Don't send me emails until my computer is fixed." → *She **asked** her friends not to send her emails until her computer was fixed.*

Other reporting verbs with this pattern include:
advise, convince, encourage, persuade, and *warn.*

When we decide what reporting verb to use, we think about the purpose of the speaker's words.
"Remember to turn off your computer." = remind (*He reminded me to turn off my computer.*)
"I'll text you when I arrive." = promise (*She promised to text me when she arrived.*)

Practice

2 Change the direct speech into reported speech, using a suitable reporting verb. Remember to make changes to pronouns and time expressions where necessary.

1 David: "I wonder if your friends are coming."
   David wondered if my friends were coming.

2 Sarah: "Can I borrow your laptop tomorrow?"

3 Jhumpa: "Download these photos to my cell."

4 Martin: "Remember to take your laptop."

5 Juan: "I'll connect you to the Internet tomorrow."

6 Lin: "Come and stay with me next week."

7 Adam: "I realize that I was wrong last night."

8 Martina: "Where are you going on Saturday?"

UNIT 12

should have and *could have*
Form

should (not) have + past participle
*They **should have gone** with a guide.*
*We **shouldn't have camped** in such a remote area.*

could (not) have + past participle
*We **could have had** an accident!*
*You **couldn't have run** any faster.*

We form the passive with *been* + past participle.
*They **should have been warned**.*
*We **could have been eaten** alive!*

Use

We use *should have* to talk about a correct thing to do in the past, which we didn't do.
*We **should have taken** our flashlights (But we didn't.)*
*I **should have brought** the first aid kit. (But I didn't.)*

We use *could have* or *might have* to talk about something that was possible in the past, but that didn't happen.

*We **could have set up** camp by the trees.* (But we didn't, we set up camp somewhere else.)

*We **might have had** an accident when that boy ran into the road.* (But we didn't.)

We use *shouldn't have* to talk about something that was wrong to do in the past, but we did.

*We **shouldn't have come** this way.* (But we did.)

*He **shouldn't have spoken** like that.* (But he did.)

We use *couldn't have* to talk about a lack of ability in the past, something that was impossible to do, and that didn't happen.

*You **couldn't have done** anything about it.* (It wasn't possible for you to do anything.)

*She **couldn't have avoided** riding through the river.* (It wasn't possible for her to avoid it.)

Practice

1 Complete the sentences with *should (not) have* and *could (not) have* and the past participle of the verbs.

1 We ___*should have eaten*___ (eat) that fruit—I'm really hungry now.
2 You _____ (tell) anyone about it! It was supposed to be a surprise.
3 It was a very dangerous situation. They _____ (get) hurt.
4 He had a very long time to do his research. He _____ (come) up with better results.
5 Do you think we _____ (ask) a guide to come with us? Then we wouldn't be so lost.
6 He didn't travel to the area, so he _____ (take) this photo.

Third conditional

Form

We form the third conditional using:

If + past perfect, *would have* + past participle

*If we **had planned** the trip, we **would have reached** our destination more quickly.*

*We **wouldn't have been** late if you'**d checked** the schedule.*

We can also form the third conditional with *could* and *might* instead of *would*.

*She **could have visited** Cuzco if she'**d gone** to Peru.*

*If you'**d eaten** that, you **might have gotten** sick.*

We can use *if* in two positions:
- *If*-clause first: *If we had planned the trip, we would have reached our destination more quickly.*
- Main clause first: *We would have reached our destination more quickly if we had planned the trip.*

When the *if*-clause is at the beginning of the sentence, we use a comma to separate it from the main clause.

Use

We use the third conditional to talk about situations in the past that did not happen, and the hypothetical result. The situation described is often the opposite of what actually happened.

*If I **had seen** him, I **would have said** hello.* (I didn't see him and I didn't say hello.)

*If I **had traveled** abroad, I **would have taken** my passport.*

Note that the contracted form of both *would* and *had* is *'d*. Don't confuse the two forms. *Had* is followed by a past participle:

*If I'**d seen** him,…* = *If I **had seen** him,…*

Would is followed by *have* + past participle: *I'**d have said** hello.* = *I **would** have said hello.*

We can use *could/might (not) have* to speculate on a possible consequence of the imagined past situation.

*If he **had asked** for directions, he **might not have gotten** lost.*

Practice

2 Complete the sentences with the past perfect and *would have* + past participle.

1 If you ___*had driven*___ (drive) more slowly, you ___*wouldn't have had*___ (not have) an accident.
2 They _____ (find) the camp if they _____ (not lose) the map.
3 _____ you _____ (plan) the trip better if you _____ (know) about the problems ahead?
4 If the explorers _____ (prepare) better, they _____ (succeed).
5 The local people _____ (be) friendlier if we _____ (understand) their language.
6 What _____ you _____ (do) if they _____ (attack) you?
7 We _____ (not feel) nervous if we _____ (read) about their customs first.
8 If she _____ (want) to come with us, we _____ (welcome) her.

Unit 1

🎧 1

A: Do you want to do this quiz?

B: What's it about?

A: Colors and what they mean around the world. For example, look at this photo. Where are the women going?

B: I don't know. To a party?

A: No, they're guests at a wedding in India. The guests and the bride herself wear bright colors like these red and orange clothes. OK, here's your next question. Does red have different meanings in Eastern and Western cultures?

B: Yeah, I think it does. I always associate red with strong emotions like love, or passion or anger.

A: That's right. And in Eastern cultures it means luck and prosperity. Oh, and courage too, it says here. OK, next: Where does yellow symbolize wisdom?

B: Well, a yellow jersey means the winner of the Tour de France to me! But I don't see the connection with wisdom.

A: Well, there are two options. Is it China or India?

B: I think it's… oh, India.

A: Let's see… yes, you're right, it's India. It means both wisdom and knowledge in India, actually. And in China, it's a symbol of power.

B: Well, I didn't know that. What's the next question?

A: OK… which color means "happiness" in Japan? Orange or pink?

B: Oh, I know this. I think it's orange. It's happiness and love.

A: Yes, it is! Well done! Amazing!

B: Are there any more questions?

A: Yeah, the last one is: Who uses green as their symbol? There are two options, but I'm not going to tell you them—it's too easy.

B: Green? Something to do with nature? Oh yes, environmentalists, conservationists, that kind of thing.

A: Of course! Now, here's a quiz all about the color green. Do you want to give it a try?

🎧 2

1 Do you want to do this quiz?

2 Where are the women going?

🎧 3

1 Where does yellow symbolize wisdom?

2 Is it China?

3 What's the next question?

4 Are there any more questions?

5 Do you want to give it a try?

🎧 4

1 **P:** Good morning! Allow me to introduce myself. I'm Paola Jimenez.

C: How do you do? My name's Colin Burke.

P: It's a pleasure to meet you, Colin. I see you work for an advertising agency.

C: Yes, umm… Paola. I'm the art director at Arrow Agency. I mostly work on web advertising.

P: That sounds interesting.

C: It is. We're developing some really new ways of advertising. Do you use the Internet much in your work?

P: I do, actually, Colin. I'm in sales. I work for an electronics company and we're starting to sell online.

C: Really? Well, Paola, why don't I give you my card? Here you are.

P: Thanks. It's been good talking to you. Let's stay in touch.

2 **L:** Hi, how are you? I'm Lucy.

Y: I'm very pleased to meet you. I'm Yuvraj Singh. I work for Get Fit. It's a chain of gyms.

L: Oh yes, my brother goes to Get Fit.

Y: Does he? Great. We're building a big new gym downtown. It's nearly ready to open, in fact.

L: Is it? That's great.

Y: Yes, we're all really excited about it. Umm, what about you?

L: Well, I'm looking for a new job, actually.

Y: OK, well, thanks for your time. Let me give you my card. Don't forget to check out our new gym when it opens.

🎧 5

1 **Colin:** I mostly work on web advertising.

Paola: Do you?

2 **Paola:** I'm in sales.

Colin: Oh, are you?

3 **Lucy:** Oh yes, my brother goes to your gym.

Yuvraj: Does he?

Unit 2

🎧 6

M = Manny, I = Isabella

M: You've just heard a very lively and energetic track from Manu Chao and you're listening to Global Music with me, Manny Ramirez. Our studio guest today is Isabella Rey. She's an expert on world fusion—that's music which mixes influences from several countries. Isabella, tell me about Manu Chao, because he's a very successful artist, although he hasn't been as successful in the English-speaking world yet.

I: No, indeed he hasn't. But Manu Chao is a perfect example of a truly globalized, 21st-century artist. His origins are Spanish, but he's lived in France for most of his life. He sings in six languages: French, Spanish, English, Galician, Arabic, and Portuguese.

M: That's an amazing range!

I: Yeah. It shows the influences that exist in his music. He mixes in all sorts, from punk, rock, salsa, and reggae to ska and raï. He's hugely successful in Europe and Latin America, but as you say, he hasn't had a big impact in this country yet.

M: So he's a good example of world fusion music?

I: Yeah. Paul Simon's another example. He's worked with Zulu artists Ladysmith Black Mambazo and several other African musicians. In fact, world fusion music has become better known since the 1986 release of Paul Simon's album *Graceland*.

M: That was a fabulous collaboration. We've got a track from that album coming up later in the show. And, of course, what about WOMAD?

I: WOMAD—that's World of Music and Dance—is a great example of how different musicians from around the world have been able to meet and influence each other. The British musician Peter Gabriel was the founder and he's been a big part of it for many years now—since the 1980s. These days, we've all heard of the incredible Senegalese singer, Youssou N'Dour—basically he's become popular outside of Senegal since his collaboration with Peter Gabriel. But he's not the only one, of course.

M: And what's happened since then, since the 80s, in terms of world fusion?

I: Well, we've seen younger musicians mix things like punk, new wave and hip-hop styles with non-Western styles to create dazzling new sounds. Like Manu Chao, as we've heard, and also Zap Mama, a new band from Belgium. They've already had several international hits. Their lead singer, Marie Daulne, has a beautiful and powerful singing voice.

M: Well let's listen to Zap Mama. This track is called "Show me the way."

7

L = Lesley, R = Richard

L: Do you feel like going out tonight?
R: Sure, why not? We haven't been out for ages. What's playing?
L: Well, there's a movie about climate change. Do you like the sound of that?
R: No, not really. It doesn't really appeal to me. What's it about? Just climate change?
L: I think it's about how climate change affects everyday life. I wonder how they make it entertaining.
R: Well, it sounds really awful. It's an important subject, I know, but I'm not in the mood for anything depressing. What else is playing?
L: There's a flamenco festival.
R: Oh, I love dance! That sounds really interesting.
L: Apparently it's absolutely superb. Let's see what it says in the paper: "Ana Gómez leads in a thrilling production of the great Spanish love story *Carmen*."
R: Great. What time is it at?
L: At 7:30.
R: Well, that's no good. We haven't got enough time to get there. Is there anything else?
L: There's a comedy special.
R: Where?
L: It's at the City Theater. It's a kind of comedy marathon for charity with lots of different acts. It looks pretty good. The critic in the local paper says it's the funniest thing he's ever seen. It says here: "Jackie Chan is absolutely hilarious as the embarrassing host to a night of comedy gold."
R: Hmm, I'm not crazy about him. He's not very funny.
L: Are you sure you feel like going out tonight? You're not very enthusiastic!
R: Maybe you're right. OK, let's go and see the flamenco—but tomorrow, not tonight.
A: Great. I'll go online and book the tickets.

8

1 It sounds really awful.
2 That sounds really interesting.
3 Apparently, it's absolutely superb.
4 It looks pretty good.
5 Jackie Chan is absolutely hilarious.
6 He's not very funny.

Unit 3

9

[Use young female voice for first paragraph and young male voice for second paragraph]

1 I live in Zambia and we have fantastic river systems here. I love rafting on the Zambezi River. It's one of the best white-water runs in the world. On my very first trip, we had a real surprise! We were coming down fast from a section of rapids and we could see calm water ahead. Then I saw a big hippo near the river bank. It's best to avoid hippos if you can! We started paddling away quickly because it was coming towards us! We were going around a small island in the middle of the river, when suddenly…

2 I began diving when I was about 12. I actually learned to dive on vacation in Mexico. My parents went there to explore the underground lakes—or cenotes. My brother and I were sitting around on the beach, getting bored, so we took a diving lesson. Then we did our first dive in the "easy" cenotes while my parents were exploring the dangerous stuff. It wasn't deep underground and the sun was shining in through an opening in the roof of the cave. It was really calm and beautiful. I felt like staying there all day! I was concentrating on doing everything right. I didn't notice that…

10

1 We were going around a small island in the middle of the river, when suddenly we surprised an 18-foot-long crocodile. It was lying in the sun on the other bank. It jumped into the water about three feet away from our boat and soaked us all. Fortunately, he didn't catch up with us!

2 I was concentrating on doing everything right. I didn't notice that I was swimming into an area that was only for advanced divers. There were ropes and signs to stop you from going into a sort of labyrinth of tunnels where it was easy to get lost. Luckily for me, my mom realized pretty quickly that I was missing and she came after me. I still had no idea!

11

1 A: Did I ever tell you about the time we had a lot of animals? Our house was a zoo.
  B: No, I don't think so.
  A: Well, among other things, we had these goldfish—they were really huge. And they lived in a fish tank above the kitchen sink. But these two fish were really active—they loved to jump in the air. Especially when someone was doing the dishes.
  B: No way!
  A: Seriously! After we saw it the first time, we put a lid across the top of the tank. So, a couple of weeks later, I came into the kitchen one morning and the tank was empty. No fish!
  B: Oh, no!
  A: Oh, yes! During the night, the fish had jumped out of the tank! They were lying in the sink! Fortunately, there was some water in it!
  B: That's incredible!
2 C: I remember once, a couple of years ago, we were looking after this friend's parrot when he was on a business trip. Anyway, after a few days, I realized that this parrot knew how to open its cage.
  D: Really?
  C: Oh yes! It happened a couple of times. When I went out, the parrot was in its cage. And when I got back home, it had gotten out. So one day, I was at work when all of a sudden I remembered that I hadn't given the bird food and water. I immediately rushed back home and there it was: the empty cage again. I searched everywhere. I was going around the house calling "Polly! Polly, here Polly, Polly!" But I couldn't find it.
  D: What happened then?
  C: Well, the next thing was, I started to panic. So I went into the kitchen to make tea, and guess what? There was the bird. It was taking a bath in my teacup!
  D: That's unbelievable!

12

1 Especially when someone was doing the dishes.
2 They were lying in the sink!
3 We were looking after this friend's parrot.
4 I was going around the house calling "Polly!"

Unit 4

13

1 Devi is from West Sumatra in Indonesia

D: I didn't stay in school because generally girls don't here. But then I got this job. I'm the first girl in my family to work outside the home. Since the economic crisis, more women have jobs. I feel very different about my future now. I'm not going to stay in this job forever. I want to be a nurse, so I've applied to college. I hope to get in. I'm taking the entrance exam next month. I'm very nervous about it. I haven't told my boss, but I suppose I'll tell him soon.

2 Elisabeth is from Bruges in Belgium

E: I work in a factory. It's a good job, but the company is laying people off so I'm going to take the early retirement package because it's an opportunity to start again. I got married very young and had a family, so I didn't finish my education. But I've just finished evening classes in business administration, and now I'm going to start my own business. It's something I already do as a hobby. I make specialty cheeses. Just a moment, I'll get you some… Here you are, taste this. Do you like it? Well, I'm meeting the bank manager on Wednesday to discuss my business plan. And hey, maybe I'll take some cheese for him to taste as well!

3 Sahera is from Kabul in Afghanistan

S: It's very difficult to study at the college level here. Many girls get no education at all. But I have managed to complete my degree and graduate from the department of language and literature. Now I'm thinking about the next step. Many of the graduates are going to work as teachers. My friend is going to continue her studies in the United States. I'm going to stay here in the city, because my family is here. I guess I'll take some time off and visit my parents. And I want to spend time with my friend because she's leaving next week.

14

R = Raaj, M = Mani

R: This looks interesting—this research assistant job for a TV company.

M: I know. The only thing is the experience. They want two years, but I've only worked part-time for a year, really.

R: One or two years' experience it says, and anyway you meet the other requirements. You're good under pressure and with deadlines—you always hand your essays in on time at college!

M: I'm not sure that's the same thing.

R: Of course it is! And you're really well-organized, hard-working, highly motivated…

M: OK, OK, if that's what you think. Is it all right if I give you as my reference?

R: Hmm, I'm not sure about that. I don't think you can just put down your friends' names.

M: I know, too bad! But seriously, do you mind helping me with my resume? I need to make it look a little more professional.

R: Of course I will. Are you going to apply for this job, then?

M: Yeah, I think I will. But I'll need my resume anyway, whichever job I apply for.

R: OK, print it out and I'll take a look at it.

M: Will you be able to do it today?

R: Yes, I will. But what's the hurry?

M: The deadline for applications is in a couple of days. Oh, can you have a look at my cover letter too?

R: Have you already written it?

M: No, but I'll do it this afternoon and then I can send everything off tonight. Hey, they might ask me to go for an interview this week!

R: Yeah, they might.

M: But I haven't got any good clothes! Would it be OK to borrow your suit?

R: Sure, no problem.

15

M: Will you be able to do it today?

R: Yes, I will.

Unit 5

16

Conservationist Mike Fay is somewhere in central Africa. He's in the middle of the longest walk of his life—so far! Fay is traveling almost 2,000 miles through the dense forests of Congo and Gabon. He's lived in the area for several years and he's worked on various forest conservation projects there. Now Fay and his team are making a record of the region's ecosystems and wildlife, especially in the unexplored and unexploited areas. Traveling through untouched forest and down wild rivers to remote villages, they can only travel on foot or by boat. They've completed about half of the route. The trek will take about fifteen months to complete, through what Fay calls "the last wild place on Earth."

17

1 The WCS has financed the work.
2 The trip has taken longer than expected.
3 The team members have worked hard.
4 The results have surprised us.
5 The project has been a great success.
6 The government has helped the project.

💿 **18**

1 L: Hi there, I'm Li.

 M: Hi, I'm Matt.

 L: Is this your first time here?

 M: No, actually. We've been coming here for about four years now. We come every July.

 L: Oh, it's strange that we haven't bumped into each other before now.

 M: Really? How long have you been coming here?

 L: About six years. We love it. There's so much to do here—that's why we keep coming back.

 M: I know, and the nightlife's awesome!

 L: I always tell everyone at home it's got everything you need for a vacation—great beaches, perfect weather, and lots to do. Are you going to the barbecue later on?

2 M: Hi, Rosa! What a surprise! How long have you been here?

 R: Matt! Hi! Oh, we just got in yesterday.

 M: Good to see you again!

 R: Listen, we're staying at the SeaView this year—the food is absolutely fantastic there.

 M: The SeaView? A few miles up the coast? Isn't that a little remote? And expensive!

 R: Well, I've been working really hard recently. I needed a relaxing, peaceful break this year.

 M: You're getting old!

 R: I know, tell me about it. I'll be 30 next year!

3 P: OK, we're ready to go. Are you nervous?

 M: A little. But I like to try something new every vacation. I always have great memories to look back at when I get home.

 P: I know what you mean. Well, sky-diving is one experience you won't forget!

 M: So Ping, how long have you been sky-diving?

 P: Oh, for quite a few years now. I qualified as an instructor five years ago.

 M: How long did that take you?

 P: Well, you need to do a minimum number of jumps before you can start the training course. It took a while! But you know, it's a great job. You can travel all over the world and find work.

 M: So what do you do for a vacation, then?

 P: I meet up with friends. We like a little excitement—New York, Rio de Janeiro, Moscow, you name it!

💿 **19**

1 T= female tourist, G = tour guide

 T: I wonder if you could help us. Our luggage hasn't arrived.

 G: Right. Are you with ChinaTimes tours?

 T: Yes. Mr. and Mrs. Wong.

 G: And which flight were you on, Mrs. Wong?

 T: The ChinAir flight from Beijing. I think it's CA2498. We've been talking to some of the other passengers and their luggage has come through, no problem.

 G: Ah, yes. It seems some bags have gone to another airport. Flight CA2498?

 T: Yes, that's right. Do you know where our bags have gone to?

 G: Yes, I'm afraid the luggage has gone to Shanghai.

 T: Shanghai? Well, how did that happen?

 G: I'm not sure, but all the missing bags are coming on the next flight.

 T: But when's the next flight?

 G: It's tomorrow morning. Don't worry, we'll arrange everything. Which hotel are you staying at? Your bags will go there directly.

 T: But all our summer clothes are in the suitcases…

2 T= male tourist, G = same tour guide

 G: Hello, Mr. Biswas. Is anything wrong? Can I help?

 T: Well, it's about my wife, actually. She hasn't been feeling well for a couple of days.

 G: I'm sorry to hear that. Is it something she's eaten, do you think? Or just motion sickness?

 T: I don't know. She's had a temperature all night, but she feels cold.

 G: Hmm. Have you both been taking anti-malarial tablets?

 T: Oh, yes. But the hotel hasn't provided mosquito nets. And they haven't been spraying the bedroom at night, either.

 G: OK, how long has she been feeling like this?

 T: A couple of days? Yes, since the boat trip on Tuesday. Is there anything you can do?

 G: Well, it's probably nothing to worry about. But I'll ask the hotel to call a doctor, just in case.

 T: That's great, thank you.

💿 **20**

1 Do you know which airport our bags have gone to?

2 Yes, I'm afraid the luggage has gone to Shanghai.

💿 **21**

1 Which hotel are you staying at?

2 Are you staying at the Ocean Hotel?

3 Where have you traveled from?

4 Why haven't we heard from the airline?

5 What have we been waiting for?

6 Are you waiting for the manager?

Unit 6

💿 **22**

1 A: I've never tried durian. Have you? Apparently, it tastes much better than it smells.

 B: No, I haven't tried it. But I know that it smells so much that you're not allowed to take it on buses in Singapore.

2 C: I feel a little sick. I wonder if it was the mayonnaise on my salad?

 D: Was it fresh mayonnaise? You should avoid using raw eggs in mayonnaise, you know. They can make you sick.

3 E: What's fugu? F–U–G–U?

 F: Oh, I know what it is. It's a kind of fish they eat in Japan. It's actually poisonous, so only qualified chefs are allowed to prepare it in restaurants. If you eat the wrong part, it can kill you!

4 G: Can you eat shark meat?

 H: Yes, it's popular in lots of countries. Sometimes you have to ferment it first because the fresh meat is bad for you. That's what they do in Iceland. It's called *hakarl* there.

5 I: I love eating oysters, but I can never remember when it's safe to eat them.

 J: The rule is you can't eat them in the warm summer months, but I don't know why.

6 K: Are you going to boil those potatoes like that, without peeling them?

 L: Yeah, why? You don't have to peel potatoes before you boil them.

 K: Yes, you do. At least that's what we do in our house!

7 M: Are you making chilli con carne?

 N: Yes, but the recipe says red beans must boil for fifteen minutes or they aren't safe to eat. Do you think that's true?

8 O: What's this on the menu? Steak tartare? Is that raw steak?

 P: Yes, you can eat steak raw. It's cut into very thin pieces. You should try it.

💿 **23**

1 You're not allowed to take durian on buses in Singapore.

2 Only qualified chefs are allowed to prepare fugu.

3 You have to ferment *hakarl* first.

4 You don't have to peel potatoes before you boil them.

24

L = Lin (female), J = Jack

L: Hi, Jack. Have you read this item on imaginary eating?

J: Hi, Lin. Yes, I saw it this morning. What a bunch of garbage! I've never heard anything so ridiculous. If we think about eating food, we'll lose weight, it said.

L: Not exactly. It said if you think about eating food, you stop wanting to eat it so much. So if you don't eat it, then you might lose weight. I thought it made sense.

J: No, it's nonsense. I'll believe it when I see it! You can't "think yourself thin."

L: Well, I'm not so sure. I think willpower is really important, especially where food is concerned. Imagine you're overweight and you want to lose a few pounds. If you don't train your mind, you won't be able to lose weight. I think you can achieve anything if you believe you can do it.

J: You mean like "mind over matter"? Well, OK, mental attitude is important when you're trying to change something in your life. But I don't think that's the same as what the news item said. So are you going to do this imaginary eating thing, then? Do you really think it'll work?

L: Yeah, why not? I won't find out unless I try.

J: So what exactly are you going to do?

L: OK, let's think. I eat too many potato chips and snacks, right? So, when I want to eat a snack, I'll try just imagining that I'm eating it. Hey, you know what? This could be amazing. I'll never have to buy chocolate again if this technique works!

J: Well, I can't believe my ears!

L: Hey, as soon as it starts working, I'll let you know. Self-confidence, that's what's important.

J: I'm going to buy you some chocolate just in case. I think you'll need it.

25

W = Waiter

W: Are you ready to order?

A: Umm, not quite.

W: No problem. Would you like something to drink while you decide?

A: Yes, please, just water's fine for now.

B: Oh, this menu looks interesting. I love trying new dishes. What are plantain fritters?

A: Well, plantain is a kind of banana and a fritter is a fried dish—in this case, fried mashed banana balls.

B: Do you mean like a sweet dessert banana?

A: No, plantain is a type of savory banana you eat as a vegetable. It's quite a bland flavor, really.

B: OK. What about akkra? What's that made from?

A: It's made from a kind of bean called blackeyed peas. They're fritters too.

B: Hmm. What do they taste like?

A: Well, akkra's usually pretty hot and spicy.

B: Sounds good! I think I'll try that. Now, what's this—ackee and saltfish?

A: Where's that?

B: In the entrees, at the top of the list.

A: Oh yes. I think ackee's a kind of fruit that's traditionally served with saltfish.

B: And saltfish?

A: That's dried salted cod. You have to soak it in water before you cook it, but then it's a bit like fresh cod. It doesn't taste salty when it's cooked.

B: OK. I might try that. What are you going to have?

A: I can't make my mind up. Oh, here comes the waiter again.

W: Can I take your order now?

A: Yes, please. I'll have the akkra to start.

B: And I'll have the same.

W: And for your entree?

A: I'd like to try the ackee and saltfish. Does it come with vegetables?

W: Yes, with plantain.

A: And how's that cooked? Is it fried?

W: No, it's boiled.

A: OK, that sounds fine.

W: And what about you, sir?

B: Can I have the goat curry, please?

W: Certainly.

A: I've never tried goat.

B: You can try some of mine when it comes. It's like lamb, but the flavor's a little stronger.

A: OK, great.

Unit 7

26

1   As an architect, I'm interested in all aspects of house design. But we can learn so much from traditional constructions and designs. They're usually the ones that are much better in bad weather conditions, and they are much more appropriate to people's needs. If you live in a flood zone, it makes sense to build your house on stilts, doesn't it?

2   Well, a shelter is something less permanent and more basic than a house. Things like the ice igloos that people build in the Arctic region, or brush huts in tropical areas, are perfect for specific needs—like when you are hunting, for example— because you can put them up quickly. The purpose of a shelter is to protect you from the elements, whereas a home has several spaces with different functions.

3   Ah yes, a ger combines elements of both a shelter and a home. It has a fireplace and maybe a chimney or at least a smoke-hole, and separate areas for men and women. It isn't as solid as a brick or stone house but it's certainly easier to take down and put up, which is what nomadic people in Mongolia need.

4   Usually the most important thing is the local climate. You know, if you live in Turkey, why build a house under the glare of the hot sun if you can adapt a cool cave? Cave houses are some of the oldest homes known, and they're a lot less basic than you might imagine. They're the best solution in really hot climates. Of course, the colder the climate, the warmer your house needs to be. Central heating, especially when combined with energy-efficient windows, heats buildings more efficiently than open fires.

5   Well, modern homes are fairly similar wherever they are in the world, which doesn't necessarily mean that they are the best design for every situation. And in our crowded cities they're getting smaller and smaller. I think, even with a modern home, you should make sure the design is the most appropriate for your climate and your needs.

💿 **27**

1 Oh, well, it's great for us because it's so much cheaper than a house. And we're all students. We don't have as much money as people who are working. Plus, renting is easier and simpler than actually buying a place.

2 Actually, it's really good because I don't have to worry when things break or go wrong. Everyone in the complex pays an amount each month for repairs and stuff.

3 We don't have anyone living right above us, so it isn't as noisy as our old place.

4 I love having a garden, don't get me wrong. But it's a little dirtier than a balcony, especially with kids and animals running in and out all day! I can't keep the place as clean as I'd like to because I have a full-time job so I don't have a lot of spare time.

💿 **28**

1 We don't have as much money as people who are working.

2 I can't keep the place as clean as I'd like to because I have a full-time job.

💿 **29**

A = realtor, C = female customer
A: Good morning.
C: Hi, I'm interested in any properties you have downtown.
A: OK, and is that to rent or to buy?
C: Oh, it's to rent. I've just started a new job here, so I think I'd rather rent than buy, for now anyway.
A: Sure. Well, we have quite a few apartments on our books, from studios to four-bedroom apartments.
C: I'd prefer something small, but not too small. I imagine I'll get a lot of friends staying with me. So, two bedrooms, and preferably with an elevator. I bike a lot and I don't want to carry my bike up lots of stairs!
A: Well, most of the modern buildings have elevators, but a lot of the properties downtown are quite old. Would you rather look at new places or older ones?
C: I don't mind—at this stage I'm just getting an idea of what things are like here.
A: OK... so you're new to the area?
C: Yeah, I lived in a small town near the mountains until recently.
A: Oh, that sounds lovely.
C: To be honest, I prefer cities to small towns. The problem with a small town is that everyone knows your business. Maybe I'm unfriendly, but I like the way the city is more anonymous.
A: Ah yes, I've heard a few people say that! I have to say I prefer living here. I suppose I like my privacy too. OK, umm, what about garage space? Do you need that?
C: No, I don't have a car. I prefer to walk or bike. It keeps me in shape.
A: Of course, you mentioned your bike!
C: Yeah! And anyway, in my experience, driving downtown is a nightmare!
A: I know, and it's getting worse. OK, well, the next thing to consider is your budget and the rental period.

💿 **30**

Would you rather live in a town or a village?

💿 **31**

1 Do you prefer playing soccer or basketball?
2 Would you rather have tea or coffee?
3 Do you prefer summer or winter?
4 Would you rather go by car or by bike?
5 Do you prefer English or French?
6 Would you rather eat fish or meat?

Unit 8

💿 **32**

1 At certain times of the year in the Arctic circle, the sky looks as though it's on fire. The colors are so vivid—like neon street signs—that you think they can't be natural. You imagine that they must be man-made and that someone must be projecting disco lights into the sky. And yet they are completely natural. In the past, people thought they might have a religious significance, and more recently scientists speculated that they could be a form of radiation. So what exactly are these lights? We now know that they are the result of particles in the Earth's atmosphere colliding with each other. The colors come from different kinds of particles. When the particles are mainly oxygen, the sky looks green. If you see a lot of red, on the other hand, that comes from nitrogen.

2 This might be a painting or a work of art. There's something very composed about it. It looks as if the green spiral is holding the orange ball. Or it might be protecting the ball. But look carefully—the amount of detail is incredible. That's because it's a close-up—or macro—photograph. It shows a butterfly egg on the stem of a plant. Why do butterflies lay eggs in such places? They must have a reason. Scientists think that this species of butterfly may choose this spot to keep the eggs safe from ants and other predators.

3 Plants that eat animals? That can't be true… or is it? It may not seem logical, but there are indeed plants that catch insects—mostly flies, beetles, ants, and so on. But how do they do it? They must use a very special technique, because obviously they can't move and chase after things. Well, one way of catching food is to pretend to be something else. Take this Australian sundew plant. To an unfortunate insect, these shiny drops look like water. But the insect must get a nasty surprise when it tries to take a drink and gets caught on the sticky spikes. Then the plant's chemicals dissolve the insect so that it can "eat" it.

💿 **33**

The Nazca lines are enormous drawings on the ground in the Nazca desert of southern Peru. Their scale is huge: the biggest of the drawings is about 650 feet across. Most of the lines are geometric shapes, but about 70 are animal shapes such as a spider, different types of birds, a monkey, and a dog. There are human figures, too. Altogether there are hundreds of these drawings and they cover an area of about 200 square miles. The lines date from a period starting about 2,000 years ago. Basically, the marks on the ground were made by moving the reddish brown stones that cover the desert and revealing the white ground underneath. You can still see the stones along the edges of the lines.

💿 **34**

1 A: Did you hear that story about the sheep?
B: No, I don't think so. What was it about?
A: Apparently, they reflect the sun back into the atmosphere because they're so white.
B: Really?
A: Yeah, and then the heat from the sun gets trapped, so it makes everything hotter. So they think sheep cause global warming.
B: Come on!
A: Well, that's what it says in the paper today.
B: You're pulling my leg!
A: It does—here, look.
B: Hmm, that can't be right! Wait a minute… what's today's date?

2 C: Let me take a look at those twenty-euro bills for a minute.
D: Why?
C: The blue ones are no good—they're forged.
D: You're kidding me! All twenty-euro bills are blue!
C: Not the real ones.
D: Are you sure?
C: I'm absolutely positive. The girl at the travel agency told me. It was on the news last night.
D: No way! They must have made a mistake. We've just changed all this money! What are we going to do?
C: I don't know... but it is April first today…
D: Oh, honestly! I really believed you!

3 **D = daughter, F = father**
D: Dad, did you see the news about gas prices? They've gone down by almost half.
F: Oh, yeah? How come?
D: I don't know. But anyway, I put gas in the car.
F: Great! Wait a minute, did you say gas?
D: Yeah.
F: Are you serious? The car uses diesel, not gas!
D: I know, but gas is so much cheaper!
F: But, but…!
D: I'm sorry. Did I do something wrong?
F: Diesel engines don't work with gas. You must know that! Oh, this is going to cost me a fortune!
D: Dad?
F: Yes?
D: How do you suppose I managed to drive the car home? April Fools'!

💿 **35**

Oh yeah?
Come on!

Unit 9

 36

Welcome to *Money Talk*. On today's show we discuss cell phone technology and personal banking. In particular, we look at how technology allows people who have never had a bank account to manage their money using their cell phones. More and more people have cell phones these days. Did you know there are about five billion phones in the world today? But, there are a lot of people without easy access to banks, which are generally located in big towns and cities. So we are seeing lots of innovations in cell phone banking—in other words, using your cell phone to manage your bank account. An example of this is the interactive voice menu system which cell phone banking uses. Using the menu system, you can talk to your cell phone and tell it what to do with your money! Now, at its most basic, cell phone banking lets you transfer your money from one place or person to another. But now the list of things you can do from your phone is expanding into paying bills, buying goods and managing your savings account.

A new cell phone banking plan has recently begun in Afghanistan. It's a good place to see how cell phone banking works in action because the cell phone network covers every town and city. Under the new plan, the Afghan National Police has started to pay all salaries through cell phones, so the policemen don't actually receive cash. Salary payments are now made directly to each individual police officer. When a payment is made, each police officer gets a text message on his phone. He can then use his phone, via the interactive voice menus, to make payments from his salary. The new system is changing the way the economy works. The Afghan people can control their finances more easily: the cash they used to carry around is now safely in the bank.

37

1 I tried to save money to get a new phone.
2 The model I wanted cost a fortune.
3 I gave up chocolate, buying DVDs, and smoking.
4 I gave the money to my sister to take care of.
5 She told me how much I'd saved each week.
6 When I had enough, I went to buy the phone.
7 The store had a special offer.
8 I got a free upgrade with a new phone!
9 And I still had the cash I'd saved. Amazing!

38

1 I tried to save money to get a new phone.
2 The model I wanted cost a fortune.

39

1 I tried to save money to get a new phone.
2 The model I wanted cost a fortune.
3 I gave up chocolate, buying DVDs, and smoking.
4 I gave the money to my sister to take care of.
5 She told me how much I'd saved each week.
6 When I had enough, I went to buy the phone.
7 The store had a special offer.
8 I got a free upgrade with a new phone!
9 And I still had the cash I'd saved. Amazing!

40

S = salesperson, C = customer
1 S: Can I help you?
C: Yes, can I look at this silver chain?
S: This one?
C: Yes, please.
S: It's lovely, isn't it? Is it for you?
C: No, for my sister.
S: It's on sale actually; 20 percent off.
C: Oh? I like it, but it's a little heavy. I was looking for something more delicate.
S: How about this?
C: Yeah, that's great. That's just right, I think. Can she return it if she doesn't like it, though?
S: Yes, she can exchange it within ten days.
C: OK, good.
S: That's as long as she's got the receipt, of course.
C: I'll take it then. Can you gift-wrap it for me?
S: Well, we don't actually do gift-wrapping, but we have some nice gift boxes for sale, over there.
C: Thanks.
2 C: Excuse me, do you work here?
S: Yes, can I help you?
C: Well, I'm looking for a sofa that I saw on your website, but I don't see it here.
S: OK, do you have the reference number or the model name?
C: Yes, it's Craftmaster. The number is 00389276.
S: OK, let me see if it's in stock.
C: The website said "available" this morning...
S: Yes, here we are. Do you want it in red, floral, or natural?
C: Floral, if you've got it.
S: Yes, there are plenty in stock. Just give them this reference number at customer pick-up.
C: OK. What about delivery? How much do you charge for that?
S: Can you tell me your zip code? The charges go by area.
C: 33062.
S: That would be $55.
C: Wow! OK...
S: If you go to the customer service desk, they can take your information and arrange the delivery date.
C: And do I pay here or...?
S: The cash registers are over by the customer pick-up. You can pay by card or in cash.
C: Great, thanks for your help. Umm, how do I get to the cash registers again?
S: Just follow the yellow arrows.

Unit 10

🎵 **41**

P = presenter, G = guest

P: Now most of us will remember TV series like *The Bionic Woman* or *The Six Million Dollar Man*, or more recently, the *Terminator* movies, in which the characters are a futuristic mixture of technology and nature. Tonight on Channel 10, there's a fascinating documentary which suggests that this bionic future is already here. Nadene, you've seen a preview of the show.

G: Yes, Owen, and it really does seem as if science fiction has become science fact. The show follows the treatment of a woman whose arm was amputated in a traffic accident, a man who has had a full face transplant and an amazing process which actually grows human organs.

P: So it's not just looking at what medical science *might* be able to achieve, but how it's changing people's lives right *now*.

G: Absolutely. Take the woman I mentioned—the lady who injured her arm—Amanda Kitts. She's been getting treatment in a hospital where they specialize in bionics. And they've developed a bionic arm which fits onto her shoulder.

P: And what kind of things can she do now?

G: Well it's still too early to tell for sure, but the doctors are confident that she'll be able to do the normal things that we take for granted, like making sandwiches or holding a cup of coffee.

P: So bionics is great news for patients who have lost the use of a limb.

G: Absolutely. And the show shows all sorts of other bionic devices, too. There will come a time when the blind can see, the deaf can hear... Right now, it seems as if the possibilities are endless. The technology, or should I say biotechnology, already exists.

P: And that's on Channel 10 tonight at 9:30.

🎵 **42**

1 A: What on earth happened to you? There's blood all over your leg!

B: Oh, it's nothing. I tripped over a tree branch or something when I was out running.

A: Let me see. Oh, that looks nasty! It's quite a deep cut. You'd better wash it right away.

B: Yeah, I will.

A: You know, if I were you, I'd go down to the emergency room and have it looked at.

B: It doesn't hurt. It's just a cut, really. I'm not going all the way to the hospital for a cut on my leg.

A: Hmm, it might need stitches, though. I would keep an eye on it if I were you.

B: OK, if it doesn't stop bleeding, I'll call the doctor's office and see if the nurse is there.

A: Good, because I don't think we've got any bandages big enough!

2 C: Is my neck red? I think I've been stung or something.

D: A little, yeah. It looks a little swollen. Is it itchy?

C: Not exactly. It's painful rather than really itchy. How funny, I don't usually react to insect bites and stuff. Oooh, I'm feeling a little sick.

D: You should put some antihistamine lotion on it and see if it gets better.

C: Have you got any?

D: Yes, I'm sure I've got some somewhere. You'll have to check the date on the tube, though. I'm not sure how long I've had it.

3 E: Ow!

F: Is your wrist still hurting you?

E: Yeah, actually it is. It hurts when I move it.

F: It might be worth getting it X-rayed. It's been, what, three days now? I wouldn't just ignore it—you might have broken something.

E: No, you're probably right. But I'm sure it's just a sprain, from when I fell against the table...

F: Even so, you should get it looked at.

E: Hmm.

F: Why don't you go and see Rosana in reception? She's the first-aid person. She'll know.

E: Good idea.

🎵 **43**

A and E

cuts and bruises

sprains and breaks

wasp and bee stings

bites and stuff

go and see Rosana

💿 44

1 A: I like this Twitter travel idea.
B: What's that?
A: It's this travel journalist, Zi Chen. She goes to different places and asks her Twitter followers to suggest things to do. You know, "I've just gotten off the train in Bogota and I'm hungry. Where can I get a good breakfast?" That kind of thing.
B: OK. And then what happens?
A: And then she writes about it. It's like a travel guide by local people—they're the ones who really know what's good. It's a great idea to use Twitter for something like that.
B: I didn't realize Twitter could be useful for anything!
2 C: It says here there's an eclipse tomorrow. Did you know?
D: Tomorrow? I thought it was today.
C: No, tomorrow. We should be able to see it from here. I'm just looking at this weather blog. It's reminding people not to look at it with telescopes.
D: Yeah, I know.
C: It's really a good blog. It tells you all kinds of things.
D: I know. I've got it bookmarked.
C: Oh, I wondered if you had.
3 E: Wow, that's terrible. Have you seen this? It's bad enough to lose your job, but finding out by text!
F: I saw that story. The company sent about 200 employees a text message. They told them not to show up for work on Monday.
E: I didn't think that you could do that.
F: Me neither, but there you go…
4 G: Oh, that's hilarious!
H: Hmm?
G: You know that weird politician, the one who believes in UFOs?
H: Oh yeah, I can't remember his name, but I know who you mean.
G: He's posted a video on YouTube. He's invited "all friendly aliens" to a meeting at the Capitol.
H: No way! Have you seen it?
G: No, but there's an article about it in the paper. Look!

💿 45

1 A: It's a great idea to use Twitter for something like that.
B: I didn't realize Twitter could be useful for anything!
2 C: It says here there's an eclipse tomorrow, did you know?
D: Tomorrow? I thought it was today.

💿 46

1 A: How much did the coffee cost?
B: What? You asked me to get tea.
2 A: We need to send a text about this.
B: What? I thought you said send an email.
3 A: I'm going home now.
B: Really? You said you were staying.
4 A: I heard that story on the news yesterday.
B: You did? It wasn't in the papers.

💿 47

A = answerphone, R = Roger, S = secretary
1 A: The person you are calling is not available. Please leave a message after the tone.
R: Hi, this is a message for Raj Singh. It's about the apartment for rent, the one advertised in Town Hall. OK, uh, my name is Roger, I'm at 617-555-1212.

I'll try and call you later if I don't hear from you first. Thanks.
2 S: P and Q Associates, good morning.
R: Oh, hello. Could I speak to Jess Parker, please?
S: I'm afraid she's not in the office at the moment. Can I take a message?
R: Actually I'm returning her call. She left me a message this morning.
S: OK, I'll let her know that you called. Who's calling?
R: It's Roger Li. She has my number.
S: Well, I'm sure she'll get back to you as soon as she comes in, Mr Li.
R: OK, thanks.

💿 48

R = Raj, N = Naomi, J = Jess, S = secretary
1 R: Hi, any messages?
N: Oh, hi Raj. Yes, there were some messages for you. Umm, let's see… Anam called about the party tonight. She wants you to call her back. A woman from the bank called. She says she can't make it to the meeting tomorrow. And someone called about the apartment. He left his name, but he didn't leave his number.
T: OK, thanks.
2 J: Hi, I'm back.
S: Hi, Jess. Just a moment, there were a couple of calls for you while you were out. Suzy… she said she would call back… and a guy called Simon said he was returning your call.
J: OK, thanks. Any more?
S: No, that's all.

💿 49

1 Could I speak to Jess Parker, please?
2 Can I take a message?

🎵 50

E = Emma, B = Beth

E: The first real eye-opener I had of what life was like in the African forest was on my first-ever expedition. It was the first day and we ended up making camp early that evening. I was exhausted and I fell fast asleep immediately. About four hours later, I was awakened by a lot of screaming and shouting and the words NJOKO, NJOKO! It was the local trackers shouting. Then I heard loud trumpeting and sounds of heavy steps. Basically, we'd put our tent in the middle of a giant elephant path. We couldn't have picked a more inappropriate place! By the time I'd managed to get all my gear and get out of the tent, all of the trackers and all of the local guides had already disappeared into the night. When we came back, three of the tents were completely flattened. That was my first taste of camping in the forest.

B: A couple of summers ago we went to Siberia. We were looking for mammoth bones and tusks, and even hoping to find some mammoth mummies. We flew in on a small plane. It's pretty remote and deserted. When you land and get out of the plane, you look around and there's nothing there. And you set up your camp and there's still nothing there. And you're sitting there, relaxing, in total silence and there's nothing… Then all of a sudden, you're joined by ten million mosquitoes. I remember we made this kind of rice and fish dish for dinner, and we were sitting there, trying to enjoy it while being eaten alive by mosquitoes. We had nets over our heads, but they were totally inadequate. The mosquitoes could still bite you. And you had to take the net off in order to eat. Every time you did that, hundreds of mosquitoes landed all over your face. They got in the food as well. It was just one part rice, one part fish and one part mosquito! You could go crazy after just a few days of that!

🎵 51

1 I ate something I shouldn't have eaten.
2 I couldn't have felt any worse.
3 I should have had some medicine with me.
4 I should have taken it immediately.
5 I could have died without it.

🎵 52

1 A: Is everything OK with your food?
   B: Yes, yes, it's wonderful. But, umm, I should have told you that I don't eat meat.
   A: Oh! Oh, dear!
   B: I'm really sorry you've gone to all this trouble.
   A: There's no need to apologize—it's not a problem.
   B: No, I should have said something earlier.
   A: It's OK. I should have asked you if there was anything you couldn't eat. It's my fault. I'll make you something else.
   B: No, please don't. The vegetables are delicious and there's plenty to eat.
   A: Are you sure?
   B: Yes, really. I'm enjoying this. I'll just leave the meat if that's OK with you.
   A: Of course!

2 C: Oh, my goodness! What was that?
   D: I dropped the tray of glasses!
   C: Oh, those nice glasses from Italy?
   D: I couldn't help it—I slipped.
   C: Are you OK? Let me help you up. You are clumsy, though.
   D: Don't blame me—this floor is slippery.
   C: Yes, but if you'd been more careful…
   D: Look, it was an accident! It could have happened to anyone.
   C: I know, I know. It's not your fault. Sorry I got upset.
   D: It is a shame about those glasses, though. We haven't had them for long.

3 E: I'm so sorry to keep you waiting. The bus didn't come!
   F: Were you waiting for the number 46?
   E: Yes, it was supposed to come at five thirty.
   F: Don't worry about it—that service is terrible. It's always late.
   E: I tried to call you, but I couldn't get through.
   F: Ah, I think my phone is off! Sorry about that!
   E: Wow, I'm almost an hour late!
   F: It's OK. It's just one of those things—buses are unreliable! Anyway, you're here now and that's what matters.

Credits